# TRANSCRIPTION TECHNIQUES FOR THE SPOKEN WORD

# TRANSCRIPTION TECHNIQUES FOR THE SPOKEN WORD

WILLOW ROBERTS POWERS

**ALTAMIRA**
P R E S S
A Division of
ROWMAN & LITTLEFIELD PUBLISHERS, INC.
*Lanham* • *New York* • *Toronto* • *Oxford*

ALTAMIRA PRESS
A division of Rowman & Littlefield Publishers, Inc.
A wholly owned subsidiary of The Rowman & Littlefield Publishing Group, Inc.
4501 Forbes Boulevard, Suite 200
Lanham, MD 20706
www.altamirapress.com

P.O. Box 317, Oxford, OX2 9RU, UK

British Library Cataloguing in Publication Information Available

**Library of Congress Cataloguing-in-Publication Data**

Powers, Willow Roberts, 1943–
    Transcription techniques for the spoken word / Willow Roberts Powers.
    p. cm.
    Includes bibliographical references and index.
    ISBN 0-7591-0842-0 (cloth : alk. paper) – ISBN 0-7591-0843-9
(pbk. : alk. paper)
    1. Transcription.    I. Title. P226.P69    2005
    653′.14–dc22
                                                           2005011204

Printed in the United States of America

∞™ The paper used in this publication meets the minimum requirements of American National Standard for Information Sciences—Permanence of Paper for Printed Library Materials, ANSI/NISO Z39.48–1992.

# CONTENTS

# ACKNOWLEDGMENTS

Some years ago, Mari Atkins, then an administrator at the University of New Mexico's Santa Fe branch, suggested I teach a course on oral narrative traditions. It was a new subject for me, and I owe Mari a debt of gratitude, for it opened doors to a field that revived earlier linguistic interests. I taught several variations on this course, from oral narrative traditions to the interface of the oral and the written. What Mari began, many good students took up with enthusiasm and added to my insights, and I thank them all.

My linguistic beginnings were shaped by Larry Gorbet at the University of New Mexico. The difference between the oral and the written has always interested me, and once this book was under way, two friends and colleagues were particularly instrumental. Janet Patterson discussed almost every aspect of the book, generously shared her knowledge of speech and language (far greater than my own), provided insights from her own research and work in transcription and training, read and critiqued critical sections, and spent hours listening to and debating details in which few would have been interested. Barbara King broadened my ideas about language and communication; provided details of her own very different kinds of transcription, thus extending my perception of this work in general; and read and critiqued portions of the work.

In addition, Pat Draper, always a mentor, read and offered extensive comments on a draft of the first chapters. Marta Weigle, whose encouragement in all things has accompanied my anthropological career, helped me decide that such a book could, in fact, be useful. Nancy Nelson reviewed the final chapter to make sure I had covered different perspectives. Jillian Gaona gave me an extensive and detailed account of making a transcript very different from the kinds I make myself. Barb Jardee, of Jardee Transcription, generously described the work she does, especially the ways in which she helps clients clarify needs they did not know they had. Jane Kepp, editor, colleague, and friend, provided the superb editing every author needs and few receive. And finally, but not least, Robert Powers supported and put up with the inevitable ups and downs of the author in the heat of creation, if such a phrase can be applied to this small, practical work.

Santa Fe, January 2005

# INTRODUCTION

When I asked colleagues in ethnology what their methods were for transcribing a tape-recorded interview, many said, "Transcribe every word, then edit." But the flow of speech is a rich soup of sounds; people repeat words or truncate them, start sentences and never finish them, use nonwords with great frequency, and add hand and facial expressions as markers of meaning. Speaking is not in the least like writing. Exactly what does it mean to "transcribe every word"? And what about editing?—this implies altering the spoken word, sometimes considerably. How, and how much, should it be done? Under what circumstances is editing either expected, necessary, and right or unwise, unmethodological, and wrong?

Transcribing the spoken word is not straightforward. Below the surface of a transcript lie conceptual issues, not to mention the different reasons and needs for a transcript in the first place. Social science disciplines in particular are based on theoretical ideas about language, communication, and exchange that frame their practitioners' approaches to the role of speech. Research goals differ, and transcribing methods need to reflect those goals thoughtfully.

Language is critical in ethnology, both for itself and for its illumination of communication, culture, and society. Linguists study the nature of language, its history and change, its acquisition and grammar. Ethnographers are interested in people in their natural settings, including their speech and their perspectives on the world. Both groups are interested in language use, interaction, the construction of meaning, communication (and miscommunication), and social context. Spoken language in its social context is the focus of ethnographic transcribing and of this book. I look at actual speech in its interactive context and provide methods nonlinguists can use to reproduce it as text.

The goals of ethnographic methods—and the reason for transcripts—are to record, to illuminate, to re-present, and to facilitate analysis. A transcript is not a full copy of the original speech act, and it should never be viewed as reflecting objective reality, whatever that is thought to be. Even an audio or video recording is not a full representation of the original event. A transcript is merely a useful tool—that is, if it is a skillfully made tool.

In this book I describe methods for creating good transcripts as tools to assist research. The elements of the spoken word that appear in recordings must be identified and methodologically translated into the conventions of writing and, on occasion, appropriately edited—what a tricky phrase—for the researcher's goals. This is not for the faint of heart, nor is it, at any step of the way, "mechanical," "secretarial," or "mere drudgery"—all descriptions I've heard used. In short, I believe transcribing is skilled work that requires shared and accepted methods. Transcriptions that have no methodology are neither useful for learning what people said nor rigorous enough to serve in research.

## TOWARD A STANDARD NOTATION SYSTEM

As I write, no standard set of notations exists for presenting the spoken word, in context, for ethnographic methods. Oral historians, it is true, have worked out transcription guidelines for their own style of research. Typically, oral historians aim to produce written texts, and often they work closely with interviewees to construct the text together. This is not the same as the ethnographic goal of trying to capture the equally shared construction of context and meaning in an oral exchange. As an anthropologist trained in ethnographic methods, I think the guidelines of oral historians are not always suitable for social scientists who need to capture the quality of speech and some of its social aspects. For those whose focus is the interplay of language, environment, social structure, culture, belief, and behavior, the spoken word requires a slightly different set of methods to capture a different set of factors.

Linguists, too, have special needs and individually have created notation systems to present the aspects of spoken language that are pertinent to their analyses. Unfortunately, these systems are neither standardized nor consistent, and they are not entirely useful for researchers who require a more easily understood transcript with notations that are more transparent to nonlinguist readers. Since there is no standard notation set and no guide for ethnographers, people who need to create and quote from a transcript (if they do not invent a new set) often use linguistic notations without regard for their specialized use and often without explaining them to the reader. Although linguistic analyses justifiably demand special notations, I believe transcriptions ought to share a set of basic conventions to which special notations (which should also be consistent) may be added for specific research.

Publication style guides only add to the multiplicity of conventions. For example, the *Chicago Manual of Style* (15th ed., 457–58) says that ellipsis points are to be used to indicate both faltering speech and omissions of material from a quotation; moreover, many people use ellipsis points in transcriptions to indicate pauses. Recognizing the lack of standardization, some authors helpfully include their notation system as an appendix, as Joseph Gone (1999:415–40) did in an analysis of an oral account by a Nez Perce elder. Having a shared, published notation system that all can refer to may still mean including such an appendix, but perhaps my offering one here will launch an effort to standardize and further develop transcription notations.

I hope this guide, written for anyone who uses ethnographic methods, will be relevant to a wide range of essentially social disciplines that rely on ethnography. Indeed, I hope it will prove useful not only to researchers drawing on theoretical ideas but also to people who are not doing social science but who want to create a good transcript for other reasons. In it I outline points to consider during all phases of transcription, many of which touch on issues and concepts that have been discussed much more extensively by linguists. Principally, I address anyone who believes the spoken word needs careful attention when it is represented in a transcript. I assume that you, the researcher, will bring your own concepts, ideas, and issues to the choices I present. Your goal is to translate certain aspects of speech into writing; mine is to offer you a consistent way of doing so.

## SPEECH AND ITS ELEMENTS

Speech, stripped from its context, is problematical because the spoken word depends on context, and context is broad and various. Part of the context is an audience, that is, a person or persons who are not only listening but also present, watching, and interacting with the speaker. Also part of the context, never to be omitted, is the interviewer or researcher, who is neither invisible, neutral, nor omniscient. Transcripts are translations, and like all translations they cannot exactly reproduce the original. But like many translations they can be well-crafted forms of the original that allow for further appreciation, insights, or analysis.

Normally the spoken word is embedded in a specific environment, a set of behaviors and meanings, and it cannot always or easily be detached. Speech can give insights into this broader picture and help us understand it. Interviews are quite specific events, and researchers conduct them increasingly commonly. They have a context, or framework, that is somewhat different from those of, say, discussion groups, storytelling events, or theatrical performances. Spoken language reflects these different contexts.

## WHAT THIS BOOK DOES AND DOESN'T DO

In this book I cover the many elements that go into the transcription of recorded speech. I consider transcripts to be a ground for research and analysis, for reference and easy access. I write particularly for people who use ethnographic methods—that is, observing, listening, and asking questions—in order to explore, discover, and understand cultures, societies, and the behavior of people in groups or as individuals in the transcriptionist's own or another culture.

I cover specific points that relate to speech: pauses, pronouns, speech styles, context, performance, nonwords, gestures, "props," dialects, and languages, to list just a few. I discuss the formatting of transcripts and comment briefly on technology and professional style guides. Editing is an important, much neglected topic, and I discuss its implications. In interviews, almost everyone wants his or her speech edited; why is this? What are the social relations that come into play in editing or not editing a transcript of the spoken word? Why are we so self-conscious about how we "read" in speech and shy away in writing from the marvelous styles of the spoken word? Yet there *are* differences between speech and writing—there should be—and we need guidelines to know when these are to be observed and when edited. There are ethics involved—who controls words?—and I review them.

Ethnographic methods, now used in many disciplines, are the background for creating recordings. I don't discuss the factors that lead up to transcription, such as interviewing skills and recording techniques and equipment; for these I refer you to the excellent series "The Ethnographer's Toolkit," which describes these methods. Volume 2, *Essential Ethnographic Methods* (Schensul, Schensul, and LeCompte 1999), is particularly relevant. Volume 3, *Enhanced Ethnographic Methods* (Schensul et al. 1999), goes further, as does volume 5, *Analyzing and Interpreting Ethnographic Data* (LeCompte and Schensul 1999). These and other publications cover the techniques necessary for the work that precedes and follows transcription.

I do not discuss the ideas, concepts, and theories that ground the many different researchers who draw on ethnographic methods and the spoken word, although I describe my own orientation in chapter 1. Nor do I include any methodology for research, only for transcription. I do not cover linguistic theory, theories of speech, language, communication, discourse analysis, theories of performance, or any other theories relevant to the different researchers who might find this book helpful. Each chapter includes a few references, including works that discuss such theories. Researchers who transcribe or formulate guidelines for transcribing the spoken word will know their own theoretical orientation best and can make decisions drawing on that orientation. I have tried to lay out the methods for transcription so that researchers can find solutions for their varied needs. Those who work in less theoretical frameworks—perhaps recording family members, for example—can use this book to determine which options best fit their goals and to understand how those options make the best transcripts for their purposes.

In focusing on verbal exchange, as I do here, I do not want to exclude nonverbal communication. It, too, should be understood as part of communication. However, I do not deal with it extensively; instead, I focus on speech. I include nonverbal activities as part of context but leave to the researcher the full working out of a script that represents nonverbal communication.

## WHO NEEDS THIS BOOK?

*Transcription Techniques for the Spoken Word* is intended for anyone who uses ethnographic methods and wants to create transcripts from audio or video recordings: participant observers who record spoken material; social scientists doing applied work or research in which they record interviews, discussions, community meetings, focus group sessions, or other events; and indeed anyone who interviews others. It can be used by professional transcriptionists and by people who want to transcribe a recording but have never attempted it before. Oral historians may find the book useful, especially if they are interested in language and want to capture something of the oral nature and social context of an interview. There are many guides to the transcription of oral history, a few of which I list in the bibliography, but they tend not to focus on this aspect of interviews.

I write for those who transcribe their own tapes, those who give their tapes to others to transcribe, and transcriptionists who transcribe the tapes of others. I take it for granted that many researchers will not themselves prepare the initial transcription, a time-consuming task that requires patience, skill, and uninterrupted hours of work. Transcriptionists, however, whether professionals or students, need clear, point-by-point guidelines for transcribing recorded ethnographic material, and this book is intended to help them obtain such guidelines from researchers. The forms in appendix A, particularly, can be used to ensure that transcriptionists receive all the information they need, as well as giving researchers an efficient format in which to provide it.

## SPEECH IN TRANSCRIPTION

Language is of crucial relevance to ethnographic methods. It is a creative act, constantly generating new ways of saying the same thing, sometimes relying on familiar phrases but always adding interesting twists and new connotations. I take it for granted that language is an activity of considerable complexity, used by human beings firmly situated in concrete environments yet constantly referencing abstractions and relying on both the environment and abstract knowledge to grasp (in all senses of the word) the social event. Speech is ephemeral but substantial in effect, and it is different from, though influenced by and in turn influencing, writing. To create good professional ethnographic transcripts, we need to understand the implications inherent in the act of transcribing any speech.

I see speech as a shared construction—shared by all those involved in a situation. Human beings reach for meaning in words, actions, and the world; they assume it, create it, and struggle to obtain it. Speech is a part of other behaviors, and communication, however imperfect, is constant, though not based on speech alone. Transcribing speech requires a sense of how talk exists in a larger picture and how the meaning we make with words is built up out of our surrounding world, our knowledge, and our imaginations.

## GETTING STARTED

This practical handbook tackles what you need to know before, during, and after transcription. In chapter 1, I elaborate on why transcription methodology is necessary for ethnographic endeavors, and I describe my own conceptual and theoretical positions concerning speech, language, communication, and writing. Chapter 2 covers all the background factors you will need to consider and plan for before transcribing, including reasons for *not* creating a transcript. It also lays out the stages in creating a transcript and my recommended guidelines for formatting it.

Chapter 3 is the methodological core of the book. It covers all the elements that come into play in making a verbatim transcript: the conventions of writing, when and how to use punctuation and nonstandard spelling, and how to indicate features such as pauses, nonverbal sounds, false starts, incomplete sentences, and poorly heard words. In chapter 4, I offer guidelines on when and how to edit the transcript, how to incorporate contextual information, and how to deal with a special case, transcripts of performances. Finally, chapter 5 traverses the "social relations" of transcripts—that is, interactions between the researcher and professional or student transcriptionists, participants in the recorded event who may need to review the transcript, and future users of the transcript, for whom it may need to be indexed and archived.

Last, there are three appendixes. Appendix A consists of forms to aid in efficient decision making for transcribing. Form 1 outlines the details of transcription to be selected by a researcher, form 2 is focused on formatting, and form 3 outlines details to be given to document each transcript. These forms are designed to assist both researchers who are transcribing their own tapes and other transcribers, but the researcher should be the one to decide on and provide this information. The researcher-interviewer can and should tailor the forms to his or her own specifications. In appendix B, I list all the punctuation symbols typically used for notation systems in transcription, discuss their common uses in publications and some of their varied uses in linguistic transcripts, and offer a recommended use. Appendix C provides excerpts from transcripts by way of illustration.

The goal of this book is to outline clearly a set of transcription practices, reflecting ethnographic methods, from which you can select those that best suit your research goals. The work of transcribing is time consuming and seemingly mundane but also essential, complex, and even creative. I hope this book will clarify the need for and the use of transcription methodology and provide a useful, efficient guide to creating good transcripts for a variety of people using ethnographic methods.

# 1

# THE ORAL AND THE WRITTEN

Elmore Leonard, the author of crime novels, captures the speech of his characters with a flair for the way real speech sounds. He has clearly listened to people very carefully. His speakers use few subject nouns, words are clipped and shortened, and pronouns and prepositions barely appear, certainly not in the way formal written grammar uses them. Yet the reader grasps the meaning and revels in the characterization of speech as well as the way it builds personalities. This artful realism is nevertheless a representation: in Leonard's creatively fashioned world of talk, characters must still make themselves clear to readers (and to each other, though this is fiction and misunderstandings are either fictional devices or rare). Those of us doing transcription have to deal with real people and their spoken words. We cannot play fast and loose with the actual speech we have on tape. That speech is not at all like Leonard's carefully created if realistic dialogue. Actual speech as spoken—and captured on tape—can at times be very unclear.

Transcribing any recorded speech is a form of translation. A transcript is a written document, not a mirror of the original activity. Of course neither is the tape or video recording, but a transcript is another step farther away from the original. A transcript can be an excellent tool, but it will be only as good as the methods used to create it.

Transcribing is not as straightforward as it might seem. Speaking and writing are different, and turning the spoken word into writing requires careful thought. Should you transcribe exactly what was said or a version that might be easier to read or understand? Which is more important, content or spoken form? Meaning or style? Broken sentences or intent? How should emotion appear in the written text? To what extent should characteristics of performance be included? Can we truly capture any of these things?

9

Those of us using ethnographic methods are interested not only in obtaining information but also in context. This includes the environment in which speech takes place, the interactions that we observe and record, the style of narrative in which information is exchanged, and the ways in which things are said. We think it is important to note where and when speech occurs and how words are used—important both for understanding what is said and for taking into consideration the influence of the social context of oral exchange. But there are limits, both practical and conceptual, to how much we can include.

Transcribing is hard, time-consuming work. Many people think it is also mechanical, neither challenging nor interesting. They are, ultimately, wrong. For those of us with an interest in human beings and language, the work of transcribing broadens our experience of speech, gives the analytical mind much more to play with than the text itself ever will, and strengthens our memory for the work that lies ahead. Although researchers rarely have the time to transcribe all their recordings, I believe everyone should transcribe at least part of a tape in each project. Listening to tapes is an extraordinary extension of experience in which to begin to learn and think about issues and patterns, theories and ideas. We all talk a great deal; the opportunity to do nothing but listen is a rare treat.

## GOOD TRANSCRIPTION METHODOLOGY

A professional transcriptionist with whom I discussed methods and whose clients included oral historians and social scientists of all stripes commented that it was rare that her clients asked about her methods. She added, "I try to advise researchers that their data are only as accurate as their transcription. If you want quality research, you've got to have quality transcription." I can think of no better rationale for using good transcription methodology.

Transcription methods consist of two distinct things: deciding which aspects of speech and its context are to be transposed into writing and choosing the conventions of writing that will convey them. Good methods are based on clear principles, and I advocate following three basic ones. Transcription should put down in writing those aspects of recorded speech that are relevant to one's research and to future uses of the transcript. It should rely on consistent conventions rather than new notations created by every transcriptionist. And it should start simply and build up to the desired level of specificity.

Transcriptionists should use conventional symbols as much as possible for conventional meanings and should never reuse symbols that already have a function. Some transcriptions are intended for a broad general reader-ship; others are required for analysis and discussion within specific interest groups. These two audiences may be quite different, but this should not prevent them from sharing basic conventions on which more complex nota-tion systems can be built to transcribe specialist features for specialist readers. In working out methods for transcribing, a critical question is how one's transcriptions compare with those of colleagues. Researchers do use other people's transcripts—within or outside a discipline, now or decades later—and consistency is needed if users are to make sense of them.

Turning spoken words into text flattens speech; removes emotion, em-phasis, and tone of voice; and strips out context. Returning these elements to a text can be done—and the result may make *Merriam-Webster's Collegiate Dictionary* look slim in comparison. Moreover, some "context" may be closer to interpretation. Verbatim transcripts reflect something of real speech, but speakers edit as they go—isn't this what restarted sentences, hesitations, and stammers indicate? Nonverbal sounds are made or wrong words produced until the right word is found and triumphantly uttered, but the transcript brings it all out as equally valid. Good methodology is not going to result in an exact re-creation of the original; rather, it is a tool to help researchers focus on critical elements in their work and represent them consistently.

The question to ask is, What is the purpose of a transcript? If it is too lengthy, it is better to listen to the original sound recording. If it is too "flat," too stripped of original matter, then notes or an abstract may be more effi-cient. Your research goals and methods will help you formulate the purpose of the transcript. Doing so will in turn enable you to select the critical ele-ments at play and make decisions about them in order to create—and it is, in many ways, a creative endeavor—texts of recorded speech for use and anal-ysis. Consistency in spelling and the use of symbols—brackets, parentheses, dashes, ellipsis points, and so forth—is necessary. Speakers, however, are not particularly consistent, and you must follow their inconsistencies. Your own decisions should be consistent within a transcript, and in my opinion it is helpful if we share similar writing conventions, using those that have already been set forth in publishing.

Transcripts are shadowy representations of once-vivid speech. Inter-views, narratives, monologues, conversations, discussions, play and play act-ing, court proceedings, and storytelling in song and poetry are only some of the types of speech recorded. Each has special challenges, and following well-chosen, consistent methods can make each type of transcript useful. Paper transcripts are better than tapes for quick use and for comparison and analysis. With some small effort in methodology, they can give back the ghost of a voice, a time, an activity, even in the flattened register of writing.

## THE GOALS OF ETHNOGRAPHY

Anthropologists first developed ethnographic methods, and the success of their discipline lies in the sharing of a methodology that relies on observing by participating and on obtaining the perspectives of insiders. After more than a hundred years, ethnographic practices have evolved into a useful methodology that is by no means restricted to anthropology.

Ethnography has been defined as "an approach to learning about the social and culture life of communities, institutions, and other settings" using specific methods that include face-to-face interaction in natural settings (LeCompte and Schensul 1999:1, 9). It involves the observation of, and the attempt to understand, the way people behave or live or think by sharing their lives and activities and by asking questions. Researchers make use of ethnographic methods to learn about facets of life such as homes and families, crafts and aesthetics, illness and health, and places and events as well as people's motives, meanings, and perspectives. Ethnographers also explore and test explanations and theories through analysis and comparison.

Almost all observation, particularly the ethnographic, involves speech in a variety of forms: exchanges, conversations, interviews, discussions, performances, and narratives. Typically, people think of interviews when they consider transcribing. Indeed, interviews may be the most straightforward type of recorded speech because an interview is recognized as a formal interaction between a very few people, typically two, in a fairly constrained environment. The action, influences, and layers of interaction manifested in an interview are somewhat more limited than those in many other types of communicative events. The setting is selected for the greatest ease of hearing and recording and sometimes for the comfort of the person being interviewed. The interviewer is able to assume that he or she is, if not in control, at least able to minimize the number of confusing, real-life interruptions and interactions that take place.

Ethnography, however, is not restricted to interviews. Conversations, consultations, the deliberations of discussion groups, and the giving of instructions are also commonly parts of ethnography that the researcher may decide to record and transcribe. Anthropologists may be interested in mother–infant interactions, classroom instruction, political debates, disputes and mediations, legal hearings, community meetings, religious rituals, and many more events involving speech. Performances, too, may be recorded, and these many-layered events may require tailored transcriptions more like scripts. Informal discussions and conversations are the hardest to transcribe because they usually involve many speakers, who are not always easily distinguished by voice, and people interrupt and speak at the same time.

Real talk is fluid and fast. It depends on unspoken references and shared knowledge. In conversation, people mention known names and places without explanation and make other references by gesture or expression (themselves culturally based) to a much greater extent than they do in formal discussions. Moreover, what people literally say and what they mean are not necessarily one and the same thing, a disjunction we see when people engage in humor, irony, or silence. Each form or register of language, spoken and written, is not only distinct but has many modes. For example, everyone alters his or her speech, however slightly, to make it appropriate to a specific situation or person—or to be intentionally inappropriate. In speech, forms such as oratory, gossip, prayers, conversations with peers, and conversations with elders all have different styles. In some cultures, forms of speech vary strongly between generations and, in other cultures, between strangers.

Ethnographic methods are a means to grasp some of this complexity in order to gain a deeper understanding of human behavior, its unfolding, its cultural connotations, and its meaning to individuals. Those of us who use such methods rely on speech, among other things. We observe people and their speech in situations that are as natural as possible and make records—notes, recordings, and transcripts—of what we observe.

The range of researchers using ethnographic methods nowadays is broad, and the disciplines numerous: sociologists, medical professionals, psychiatrists and psychologists, discourse analysts, speech and language pathologists, educators, and oral historians as well as cultural anthropologists, linguists, and archaeologists. Social scientists use ethnography to try to understand behavior either within their own culture or in very different cultures and for practical, real-world goals, such as mediating conflicts between groups, designing community housing, and providing appropriate medical care. Outside the social sciences, dieticians, detectives, educators, facilitators and mediators, family genealogists, market researchers, and even corporate managers and administrators may observe or record interactions or carry out interviews, which may be enriched by including the broader perspective of ethnographic methods in transcription.

In short, researchers of many stripes rely on ethnographic methods, including the recording and transcribing of speech, to tackle practical problems and deepen their understanding of their areas of interest. To give one example, Deborah Tannen (1994) has used the ethnography of speech to write about communicative styles, particularly the differences between women's and men's speech and the kinds of speech people use in business, hospitals, and other workplaces so that we may all understand—and perhaps improve—the way we communicate.

Moreover, transcribed speech can yield new insights long after the fact. Michael Silverstein (1996) analyzed an excerpt from Edward Sapir's *Wishram Texts*, taken down in 1905 in both the Kiksht language and in English translation. By studying Sapir's transcript of a long-ago conversation on the Yakima Reservation about a particular myth and practice, Silverstein repositioned both the young student Sapir and his somewhat older Wishram colleague, Peter McGuff. He suggested that the transcript, when examined more deeply, offered telling insights into the social changes of the period and their effects on customs and relationships (Silverstein 1996:81–105). Such an analysis illustrates not only what can be done with transcripts but also the importance of having good ones in the first place.

Whether the topic is business speech, American Indian myths, psychological diagnosis, identity politics, children's language development, or family history, people record the spoken word and often need to transcribe it for ease of analysis, of comparison, or simply of reading, which is faster than listening. Court transcriptions, made by highly trained professionals using special equipment, are examples of the use—and necessity—of transcripts. These transcripts (though not easily accessible to learn from) rely on precise tools and methods to reproduce the spoken court proceedings in accurate texts for legal purposes. We should make sure that we transcribe our own ethnographic recordings with similarly good methods, and I have tried to build on the clarity of the court transcripts I have seen.

## THE THEORETICAL APPROACH BEHIND THIS BOOK

Each researcher will have a specific theoretical or disciplinary approach and a reason for recording and transcribing specific events. My goal in this book is to set out a system of transcription notations and to highlight the range of possible points to observe in speech so that every researcher can produce a transcript appropriate to his or her methods and purpose. I am a strong proponent of methods grounded in research and theory, and this guide is informed by my research experience and my approach to language and speech.

Most of the examples and almost all the references in this book come from anthropology. I am a sociocultural anthropologist, trained in ethnographic methods. This means, among other things, that I see speech as part of a broader picture, firmly set in an environment consisting of social context, time, place, setting, people, and culture. I understand speech as a complex activity that is critical to ethnography. In talking, people give hints of the world they live in, worlds that are interesting and often new to me. I want to understand them, and I want to describe and try to explain them to others as they have been explained to me. I am interested in language as it is actually spoken, the way it is used, and the social structure for which it is evidence. Most of the speech I record consists of interviews and discussions of various kinds. My work sometimes consists of research into the past and sometimes involves "applied," or "public," anthropology, geared toward practical results. Although mine is not precisely an ethnography of speaking, that is my underlying approach, and I draw on the work of Keith Basso, Alessandro Duranti, and Dell Hymes, among many others. I am interested in what people say and how they express it. Although I am interested in individuals and individual speech, my general focus is larger, a matter of social meaning and structure and the way people position and reposition themselves in talk relative to the sociocultural arena. When I interview people, I join their perspectives and their voices to those of others. Biographical details connect the interviewees to a broader story about the flavor and specifics of places and periods, of groups and events, and especially of change. These specific interests do not affect the transcription methods I offer here; rather, they affect my transcription *choices*, just as your research will affect yours. I do about half of my own transcription work and use students or professional transcriptionists for the other half.

Language, for me, is a part of culture, behavior, and society, not a separate system that exists outside human beings. We live in language, and we build it up as we go along, creating meaning with one another and changing both meaning and language constantly and subtly, in the present and over time. Speech is a crowded playing field of sounds, performances, social constraints, meanings, intentions, and cultural knowledge. Communication is varied and variable in intent; it occasionally achieves a result rather different from what we expected. Yet even a "failure to communicate" can be quite as revealing as "good" communication for unpicking certain situations. Language is as good for hiding as for revealing, for intentionally confusing as for clarifying. It can be a process of exploration or of boundary maintenance, a surface exchange or an exchange that creates meaning. Nor should we forget the role of silence. Keith Basso, an anthropologist who works among the Apache, has pointed out the ways in which "acts of silence are interpreted and the reasons they are encouraged and deemed appropriate" (Basso 1972:68). I might add that silence can also be discouraged and deemed inappropriate. Transcription relies on the spoken word, but silences in speech can be important and may need to be noted.

Speech is central to human interactions, although there are styles, places, and times in which talk is or was not salient. Currently, talk is prevalent in many cultures, spurred on by the technology of telephone, radio, film, television—even the Internet—and related to the distances we live from each other. But humans have many modes of communication, including nonverbal ones. Neither teaching nor learning is necessarily done through speech. Silence, gesture, and visual observation are also forms of communication. Human exchange varies in style and format over time and place, from wordy to parsimonious with words, from focusing on written words to focusing on oral transmission, from verbal to nonverbal and visual communication. In this book, however, I focus primarily on speech. If your work relates to body movements, gestures, or nonverbal communication generally—although I offer some suggestions for transcribing these—you will want to develop or refer to other methods (see, for example, Goffman 1983). It may be that videotape rather than audiotape will be your tool of choice.

Speech is embedded in social context: it takes place as part of actions and interactions in time and place. This context includes objects in the material world—"props"—and people, their status and relationships, and intentional or unintentional interruptions, all of which influence meaning and the interpretation of meaning. (For an overview of context, see Giglioli 1972 and Goodwin and Duranti 1992.) Speech is embedded in social situations, and we jointly construct meaning from the specifics of these interactions (Hill and Irvine 1992:2, 18).

But no work, no representation, can provide the whole picture. Speech is always an interaction of some kind, and all the speakers involved (it is worth remembering that an interviewer speaks, too) not only listen but watch and take cues from the physical, social, and cultural context. In transcribing, I think it is important continually to ask ourselves, What is relevant to *this* work? The methods I suggest stem from that question, with the understanding that, in a many-layered activity, we cannot capture everything—not even a videotape does that. Nor do we want to, virtual reality notwithstanding.

Speech is not a written text, and this seemingly obvious statement needs to be understood before one embarks on creating a text from speech. First, let me comment on the term *text* and the way I use it. The word derives from the Latin *texere*, to weave, from which we also get *textile*, and its meaning includes the notion of words, as written, in some original or authentic form. Anthropologists and other scholars have expanded the concept of "text" to include "cultural assemblages"—of ritual, oral tradition, discourse, or indeed any unit (presumably including words) that is "entextualized" for interpretation and analysis (Clifford 1988:38). This conceptualization of texts and the ensuing discussion, analysis, and critique of it have been both challenging and thought-provoking. It has led ethnographers to be more aware, among other things, of their own situation in the midst of, and affecting, whatever they observe. In this book, however, when I mention a text, I am being specific: I mean a transcript or other written document, and I usually qualify the term as "written text" for clarity.

I focus on the spoken word *as it was spoken*, but I am not a linguist. The special needs of linguists to note specific grammatical, indexical, inflectional, and other elements of speech are not covered in this book. I hope linguists will critique my notations and build on or improve them.

Finally, my approach to performance. Some theorists perceive all human interaction as performance. I tend toward a view of performance as an event framed in some way that makes it stand out. I do think of interviews and narratives (heard or recorded) as performances; they are framed, often implicitly, by both speaker and recorder. "May I interview you?" is, in my view, a device that makes the speaker fully aware of the performance being requested. If there is an audience for the event, then it is fully part of the performance. But there are many other kinds of performances as well, with various traditions and formalities. For a review of performance concepts, I recommend Ruth Finnegan's book *Oral Tradition and the Verbal Arts* (1992:91–111).


## WRITING

In order to understand the difference between speech and written documents, it is useful to know a little about writing and its evolution. Writing has been developed in different parts of the world, using different graphic systems, over at least five thousand years, not including pictorial systems. The alphabet used in the West is a system of representations of consonants and vowels that grew out of Greek, which itself came from an earlier script based on consonants developed by Canaanite speakers living in the region that is now Syria. Other alphabets with similar roots formed, changed, died, or developed as humans carried them abroad and societies rose and disintegrated. Among others, Jack Goody has a useful chapter on the development of writing in his book *The Interface between the Written and the Oral* (1987:3–56).

Early cuneiform writing was used to record quantities of goods, payments of taxes, and exchanges between merchants; to make lists of words, names, and royal genealogies; to systematize laws; and to note the movements of stars. People used writing to inform, advertise, compare, and preserve information. It was efficient, an aid to administration, and, as Goody notes, useful in the maintenance of power. Writing is a technology and like all other technologies reflects the society in which it develops. Thus, the kinds of materials people write with, their availability, and the ways people use and have access to writing and its products are always socially structured.

Whenever something is written down—whether in a trading manifest, a diary, or a newspaper article—the document has a certain concrete presence. It acquires a life of its own, surviving in a way very different from that of verbal accounts, discussions, and exchanges, even when those are clearly remembered. Though in the long run not every document survives—a good thing, no matter how much we might bemoan it—in the short term we navigate our past, present, and future through records: contracts and lists, dictionaries and histories. Writing has implications, some of which are relevant to the creation of transcripts. It is less ephemeral than speech, but it can still be lost or destroyed. As a concrete object, it can be owned and thus used, made public, controlled, and denied to others. Copying and publication (by hand, as in the Middle Ages, or by computer, as in our own time) make written documents more available; commerce and copyright control them. Both access and control have or stem from political and economic influences.

As in speech, writing, too, has a wide variety of forms: diaries, novels, poems, newspaper articles, instruction manuals, song lyrics, and term papers, to name only a few. What's more, writing can affect speech, and vice versa, in many ways, in places even where writing is not used much, in the past and in the present. Writing is almost always seen as a register requiring formality and a style different from that of speaking. This most clearly influences transcription when people review their own speech in a transcript.

Writing is thus part and parcel of current society, and it affects people (whether or not they read and write) in as many ways as does speech. Many people are unaware of the extent to which writing permeates culture, not only in the twenty-first century but for the previous few thousand years as well. Even societies that sustain and give primacy to oral communication, narrative, and traditions have been affected by foreign systems of writing, sometimes in addition to their own earlier recording systems. This point is important because it means that there is no easy splitting apart of "the oral" and "the written." They intersect.

## THE ORAL AND THE WRITTEN IN HISTORY AND ETHNOGRAPHY

As I mentioned in the introduction, oral history is the only social science discipline in which practitioners have worked out clear, consistent guidelines for transcription. Because I believe these guidelines are not always appropriate for people who use ethnographic methods, I want to discuss a bit further the similarities and differences between ethnography and oral history.

Historians explore the past, and so do many anthropologists. Both re-create it from many forms of evidence—documents, objects, buildings, landscapes, and interviews. Although oral recollections have not been history's traditional foundation, the subdiscipline of oral history was built around precisely such narratives. Ira Berlin, Marc Favreau, and Steven F. Miller, in their introduction to *Remembering Slavery* (1998), give an excellent brief account of the development of oral history, its changing procedures and approaches, and its acceptance or rejection in academe.

Awareness of the way in which oral history feeds into social history has grown among historians, and they have become more appreciative of the impressions and details of daily life, especially for undocumented subject matter and for people who did not create or appear in written documents. Oral historians now view transcripts as important documents. Their interviews need to be turned into written text, partly to facilitate research and partly to create materials for the distant future (see Baum 1995; Ives 1974; Ritchie 1995). Oral history interviews are directed, and their transcripts are reviewed and edited. These carefully crafted documents are usually jointly constructed by the researchers and the interviewee.

Ethnographers and oral historians recognize that interviewing and oral history are joint activities. For ethnographers this recognition is not merely political but also sociolinguistic and pragmatic: language is interactive, and it can make impressions on the world. The interviewer, whether historian or ethnographer, and the narrator "are both involved in creating narratives through the process of studying each other, and it is the intersection of those narratives that lies at the heart of oral history" (Grele 1985:2). It is this interaction that adds complexity to the created document, as each of several sides puts down its narrative about the past. Motives, goals, and methods differ, however, and the differences relate partly to politics, partly to disciplines, and partly to identities. Who may tell whose story?

Historians direct interviews through sets of specific questions, leading participants toward topics they consider relevant to their inquiry. Ethnographers first take part in local activities, engage in as much daily life as they are permitted to, and observe; context plays a far greater role. When asking questions or interviewing, they, too, attempt to direct some interviews (for some interesting views on the culture-bound nature of questions and interviews, see Tullio Maranhão's essay "Recollections of Fieldwork Conversations" [1992]). Another common ethnographic tool is the unstructured, open-ended interview (see Schensul, Schensul, and LeCompte 1999:135–41).

For oral historians, the interview is the foreground, and the social information the background. For ethnographers, it is the reverse: the interview is background material for an account of broader scope.

Current ethnographic methods rest on the recognition, first, that there are power relationships involved and, second, that ethnographers are not necessarily "in control." All interactions and interviews, whatever the politics of the situation, are jointly constructed—a term often used is *co-constructed*—and ethnographers participate in, influence, and are influenced by the very situation they have set out to observe. Those using ethnographic methods want a much more free-flowing picture of behavior, social groups, and people, including the style and character of speakers, with all the regional inflections, special terms, creative patterns of speech, and uniqueness that accompanies each individual voice. They may look at performance, at groups in conflict or cooperation, at individuals and their motives, at political situations, or at craft production; they always look at the cultural and social environment.

Anthropology and the ethnographic method have encouraged historians to take note of the role of culture and the idea of language. Historians have influenced anthropologists to recognize the importance of learning about the past and to adopt means for doing so. But even though practitioners in the two fields often exchange roles, each approach has its own perceptions and methods, and transcripts need to reflect this.

## METHODS REVISITED

Speech is always set in a larger context that inflects the spoken word, sometimes in obvious ways, sometimes only glancingly. As social beings, we are all aware of more than mere surfaces; as researchers, we ask questions about all the background, foreground, and middle-ground factors that play into human situations. Yet none of us can realistically produce a written script that replicates even half of this multiplication of detail. Nor would we want to; we choose what we want to put into a transcript. And for this we need methods.

Each of us, in recording an event, focuses in on some set of questions and details, even when we are aware of a fuller range of factors. In the same way, the transcriptionist relies on the purpose of the transcript to select one or another solution or option for any given element of the recording. Your speaker stammers, stops, and starts the sentence not once but twice—must you replicate this in the transcript? The question to ask is, What does this repetition indicate? Does it relate to the kinds of information the transcript is intended to include? If you are a psychologist interested in states of mind, such a repetition may be crucial, as it may be if you are diagnosing physical states or examining group dynamics, individual intentions, or communication styles. On the other hand, if you are interested in the flow of a narrative, the content of an interview, or the direction of a discussion, the repetition may only slow down the reading of the text without adding much. The goal of your work—research or applied, historical or biographical, theoretical or practical—will determine the kind of speech you record, and it must also shape the transcript you want to produce.

The following is a list of basic points that will come up for every transcription. I discuss them in the following chapters, explaining what role or meaning they can have in a transcript, options for handling them, and, where applicable, by what notations (see also appendix A).

- The verbatim (every word) transcript: a necessary first stage
- Can you omit or edit anything from the beginning?
- The conventions of writing and how to use them
- Speech, phonetics, and spelling: usage and implications
- Punctuation in transcripts
- False starts, broken sentences, and repetitions
- Filler words and nonverbal sounds
- Pauses and silence: when, why, and how to indicate them
- Overlapping speech; reported speech
- Words that are unclear or inaudible on tape
- Transcribing foreign languages
- Styles of speech, regional and personal
- When and how to handle expression and performance, drama and poetry
- To edit or not to edit: whether, when, and how to polish
- Context and editorial comments
- Reviews, relationships, ethics, and documentation
- Corrections and changes
- Future use, future preservation

When you transcribe speech, these points should be handled consistently. If you omit false starts in one place, for example, you should omit them elsewhere in order not to give a misleading weight to the one time you include them. Consistent guidelines should be laid down and followed, though never set in stone. Your notation system needs to be entirely consistent, but guidelines should not get in the way of the creative element in transcribing.

The best transcription will result from your ability to interpret the guidelines intelligently. Ask for what project or use the transcript is being created. Who will read it? How large will its readership be? Will it—or your papers—ever end up in an archive? Sound methods will help other people understand the transcript in the same way you do, to the extent that this is possible. Although the reader cannot, perhaps, have your depth of understanding—you were there, after all—the crucial elements can be passed on. Even you, returning perhaps to earlier work, may need a transcript that brings back the situation, the research, the people, and some necessary details. The methods of transcription ensure that these important details will be captured for readers and for research, perhaps far into the future.

# 2

# BACKGROUND FACTORS IN TRANSCRIBING

The work of turning a sound tape into a written document is challenging and time consuming. It requires good equipment, good hearing, and a grasp of the difference between the spoken and the written word. It helps to be quick on the keyboard and, in cases where the transcriptionist is not also the recorder, to have some contextual or local knowledge relevant to the recorded event. Methodology and efficiency in transcription are aided by some preparation and thought; it's useful to know, even before recording, what to think about before deciding or beginning to transcribe. This chapter offers an overview of the background to the work of transcribing.

## DECIDING WHETHER TO TRANSCRIBE

We make transcripts primarily for ease of access, in order to review, understand, and think about spoken words. We need no equipment to read a text, we read faster than we can listen to a video- or audiotape, and we can more quickly find what we want in a transcript than in a tape—especially if the transcript has been indexed—and ignore what we do not want. We can read and contemplate the contents; we can compare different transcripts or parts of a single transcript (does the speaker change his or her mind?). We can quote from a transcript, and different researchers can quote with consistency. We create transcripts to preserve the event because paper lasts for a very long time and, if created and stored properly, will outlive a magnetic tape recording, whether video or audio. Nothing quite replaces the original sound (and viewing) of an interview, but a written transcript is an immensely valuable additional record. It is long-lived, low-technology, and an efficient means of accessing, selecting, and using the interview's contents.

The decision to transcribe (or not) is usually made pragmatically. Transcribing an interview requires time, anywhere from three to twenty-four hours per hour of recording. Other factors are equally important: the availability of transcriptionists and funds; the question of whether participants should review the transcript and how long that might take; the clarity and audibility of the tape, especially when copied; and whether equipment for copying tapes is available. The tape's contents need to be not only comprehensible but also relevant to one's research goals and valuable for analysis. Both transcriptionists and other users need equipment to play audio- and videotapes and to create transcript documents that can not only be printed out but also, if necessary, shared across computers. Tapes and transcripts need to be stored appropriately for both the short and the long term. If the interview is likely to be used often—perhaps because it is unique or especially informative or because it is part of a set of necessary records—then transcription may be the most efficient and effective means of making it available, but future research needs should be evaluated in case it is not. For multiple or future use, the transcript might need to be indexed. Agreements, permission forms, and other ethical considerations should be in place and known by all.

Some of the practical considerations I have listed will inevitably make it difficult or impossible to make transcripts. These include lack of funds, time, or a transcriptionist; contract issues or ethical constraints; poor-quality tapes; ease of and preference for using tapes rather than written texts; and language problems. Some tapes are simply impossible to transcribe. A taped discussion, for example, might involve several people in a room, an auditorium, or even the outdoors, and their voices may be hard to hear and hard to distinguish. Even when I have been present at a discussion, if I have not made notes I sometimes have difficulty distinguishing one voice from another. A transcriptionist who was not present will find it even harder.

A good example of some tapes that were not transcribed because of such difficulties are several tapes in the John Adair archives at the Wheelwright Museum of the American Indian in Santa Fe, New Mexico. Adair recorded some discussions between Navajo filmmakers as part of a project carried out in the 1970s. He labeled the tapes with the names of the discussants, but the original quality was very poor, and the speakers were clearly at variable distances from the tape recorder. It is difficult to distinguish one speaker from another, and, of course, the listener does not know which voice belongs to which name. Adair himself could have identified them at the time, but the poor quality of the tapes makes it possible that, twenty-five years later, even he might not have been able to identify all the voices. Transcription now would be neither easy nor worth attempting.

Clarity of content, or the lack of it, is a crucial ingredient in deciding whether to transcribe an interview. I have on several occasions decided not to transcribe interviews that were confusing or provided little of the information I was seeking. For example, in a long interview with carefully constructed questions, my respondent focused on a topic of interest, anthropological theory, that was unrelated to the purpose of my interview. This is a splendid example of the influence of social context—I was interviewing a senior anthropologist—and the fact that the researcher does not necessarily control the situation. It also exemplifies when not to transcribe a tape, although the tape itself should be properly labeled and kept. Some interviews may be confusing if the interview was poorly done or the narrator used too few specific words or too many incomplete sentences. Even interviewees can have bad days.

As you weigh the issues surrounding whether to transcribe, remember that you have the option of making a partial transcription. Partial transcription has much to recommend it, especially when interview information is also being recorded in notes or other kinds of records. It has its risks—for example, of decontextualizing material or taking material out of context, which can be seriously misleading. But a partial transcript is useful when you have neither funding nor time for fully transcribing tape recordings or when there are reasons not to transcribe the full interview, such as comments on the tape about other people, discussion irrelevant to your research, or mention of sensitive topics. You can transcribe only the portion of the interview you need for your own use, which might be as little as a sentence or as much as a few pages. I've done this when an interview included something of immediate relevance to my current work but also much other information.

## THE TIME FACTOR

Transcribing audiotapes is demanding work and very time consuming. Transcribing an hour of speech takes a minimum of three hours (for an interview at which the transcriptionist was present, using a transcription machine). (Court recorders who do simultaneous transcripts are trained on special transcribing equipment.) It can demand as much as fifteen hours (for an inaudible tape in which many people are speaking, using words unfamiliar to a transcriptionist who was not present at the interview) or even twenty-four hours (for a videotape of young children's speech).

Reviewing a tape against a transcript and making necessary corrections takes roughly two hours per hour of tape (your own work or that of a professional transcriptionist), but it might require three hours or longer for transcripts with more errors. Challenging recordings take more time, according to the kind of problem or level of difficulty.

As an example, when I transcribe my own recordings, without a transcription machine, I take on average three to four hours for a one-hour interview and five to six hours for one hour of recorded discussion among several people. I have had students transcribe for me; I instruct them not to take much time with words they cannot make out, especially foreign words or names, but simply to guess how many words are involved. They average between four and five hours per hour of tape for a good draft transcript that includes some gaps and errors. My review of a student's transcript against the tape—including corrections, which I make immediately, on-screen—requires approximately two to three hours per hour of tape. I also review my own transcriptions, which takes roughly one to two hours per hour of tape.

Some conditions make transcription more difficult and thus more time consuming. For example, recordings might be made on poor equipment or made without lapel microphones when those involved are moving around or are outdoors. Videotapes in particular are challenging because in addition to speech they may involve recorded actions. Whether and how you communicate these actions in writing will depend on the goal of the research and the purpose of the transcript. Sound can be poor on videotapes (if so, acquire a set of earphones, which will help considerably). If behavior is unimportant for your purposes, it may be better to tape-record the video and then use the audiotape for transcription.

Some types of speech are difficult to transcribe, such as expressions in foreign languages that need to be translated, the words of speakers who switch between two languages ("code switching"), the speech of small children, and the words of speakers who have very low voices, who frequently change pitch, or who have unusual patterns of speech. Even speech that includes many words or pronunciations with which the transcriptionist is unfamiliar—place-names, say, or medical or legal terms—can add to transcription time.

Also affecting how long it takes to transcribe an hour of sound are factors such as the skill and experience of the transcriptionist, whether he or she is also the interviewer or was present at the interview, whether a transcription machine is used, whether the recording is audible (and, if not, whether the problem is merely very low sound or a noisy background), how fast the speakers talk, and how much overlapping speech there is.

## ETHICS

Ethical issues, which I discuss further in chapter 4, are also pertinent to the decision whether to transcribe. Each discipline has its own set of ethical protocols, including institutional review boards and other forms of peer review. Obtaining informed permission is universal for anyone who records an interview and for most other research activities as well. Your discipline or training will undoubtedly prepare you for the kinds of permission forms you need for a particular project. Two useful bulletins on ethics have been published by the Council for the Preservation of Anthropological Records (CoPAR), "Some Ethical Issues to Consider When Depositing Your Records" (Bulletin number 9), and "Ethical Use of Anthropological Records" (Bulletin number 10), and can be found at their website, affiliated with the National Anthropological Archives, Smithsonian Institution (www.nmnh.si.edu/naa/copar/bulletins/htm). The Oral History Association (OHA) website and books by Willa Baum (1995), Edward Ives (1974), and Donald Ritchie (1995) all give examples of permission forms for use in oral history projects. Permission forms usually state the purpose of the recording, make clear how it will be used, and include details about access to and publication of the audio- or videotapes and transcript, confidentiality, and public use. You and others will have to adhere to the constraints or specifics of the permission form or the research protocols of the project. Transcripts are made for easy access; they will be included in project papers, perhaps yours. If you have agreed to keep these confidential, make sure the transcript remains confidential, anonymous, removed from computer files, or shredded, for the future as well as the present.

Reviews by an internal review board (IRB) are essential for most research involving people to ensure that it is ethical and causes no harm. All such research requires informed consent and permission forms for recording of interviews, discussions, the conversations of focus groups, or similar activities. In my view, if you are interviewing and recording anyone for more than just a brief comment—regardless of your purpose, the approval of an IRB, and especially if you are an independent interviewer—you should have a short, typed permission form for those being recorded to sign.

A permission form should state that you may or will publish or archive the tape and a transcript of the interview. Transcripts involve—or can bring up—issues of intellectual property rights. By discussing beforehand the work, its results, and how they will be used, everyone concerned will be fully informed when you start to record. When on-the-spot photocopying is infeasible, have duplicate permission forms available so participants can immediately receive a copy. This is both good manners and good ethical practice, and I can think of few situations where it would be inappropriate. Every situation has its own sensitivities. Some transcripts need to be reviewed by the people involved; others do not. The agreements are specific to each recording or project. A basic rule of thumb for interview material should be that if there is no written permission (though I can think of no situation in which an interviewer would record *without* a signed permission), then there should be no transcription and no further use of the tape. If you decide to make a transcription from such an interview, it can be only for limited, one-time use.

## USING A TRANSCRIPTIONIST

Transcribing other people's tapes is challenging. People speak fluently, idiosyncratically, and often quite fast, without thinking about the creation of a document. The transcriptionist is dependent on the interviewee's tone of voice and the clarity of the recording. It helps if the transcriptionist knows a little of the context, perhaps the region or the profession or the topic, so that place-names, special terms, and pronunciations are not completely unfamiliar. However, professional transcriptionists have experience that has broadened their abilities and honed their listening skills. The interviewer can give the transcriptionist a good description of the context and should provide him or her with a list of the names of those involved, relevant place-names, and subjects under discussion.

Students can make good transcriptionists, especially if they are being trained in the area in which the research is being done. Furthermore, training in transcription will add to students' skills in methodology and provide them with experience in listening to the spoken word.

Choose a potential transcriptionist with a sense of what makes a good match for the type of recording to be transcribed. Good, clear, precise guidelines are essential. A fuller discussion on working with transcriptionists, professional and nonprofessional, comes in chapter 4.

## PLANNING AND NOTE TAKING

Certain aspects of planning the recording of an interview or other event are important to the success of a later transcription. Being prepared to take notes is one of these. Most people make notes when they are recording an event, whether it is an interview, a discussion, a symposium, or something else. Notes can be sources of contextual comments, the basis for follow-up questions, and backup resources for the tape. They can provide useful keys to topics for later indexing and helpful guides to use in locating sections of tape for partial transcription. Often, even if you, the researcher, are transcribing the tape, you may find it hard to recognize a person's voice in the recording, especially later on. Notes are necessary.

Certain events require note taking. If you record structured discussions (as well as interviews, narratives, or exchanges from one person to another), take notes on topics and who is speaking. You may want to note contextual events or expressive details as basic information. We can rarely do this for fast, fluid conversations or informal discussions. At the very least, though, make notes on who is speaking if there is more than one person.

When recording group discussions or any other group event, planning is essential. The equipment must be good, and placement of the recording device should be well planned. Designate a specific note taker—perhaps the same person who is responsible for taping and labeling or even transcribing the tapes.

A note taker should document the event: record the names of all speakers, in the order in which they speak, with the first few words they say. Asking speakers to announce their names rarely works; people forget to do it, and in many kinds of events it cannot be done appropriately anyway. Ask the note taker not to use tape counters—they are problematic because the tapes always need to be wound back as far as they will go before starting, in order to obtain the same counter for all users. However, the recording will not begin until the lead tape has ended. Set up your tapes beforehand, wound to the end of the lead tape; this ensures quick tape changes and the loss of as few words as possible. But the counters on the tape when it is being recorded will not match the tape as it is used by the transcriptionist. Plan the recording and note taking well, and transcription will be more efficient.

## THE STAGES OF TRANSCRIPTION

A transcription requires 1) a guiding principle for the speech and context to be included; 2) notation conventions—that is, ways of representing elements of speech in written form; and 3) a format for presenting the written text—both a physical form (paper, CD) and a design (the way the text appears on the page or screen). But there is one constant for all transcribing in which you want to focus on the spoken word: first obtain a verbatim transcript—that is, an accurate, word-for-word text. Whatever you may later add to or take out of this text, preparing it is a necessary first step. Exactly what a verbatim transcript consists of is tackled in chapter 3.

Transcription may have several stages, depending on the type of research, the number of people involved, and the analysis to be done. There are a minimum of two stages: initial transcription and corrected final transcription. In many research projects there are more. Researchers creating their own transcripts for their own use can make decisions and create the transcript in one step, followed by a review or proofreading. Other research may require a transcriptionist, reviews by one or more researchers, corrections, editing, review by participants, more changes, and so on, seemingly endlessly. The following is a brief outline of the stages generally involved in transcribing, showing chapters in which the topic is discussed:

1. Duplicate all the tapes to be transcribed or used.
2. Create a verbatim transcript (chapters 3 and 4; appendix A).
3. Review and correct the transcript against the tape; edit, if necessary (chapters 3 and 4).
4. Where relevant, give the transcript to others to review (chapter 5).
5. After reviewed transcripts are returned, make changes if necessary (chapter 5).
6. Record contextual information; index and archive (chapter 5).

## 1. Duplicate All the Tapes

If you do not have equipment to copy tapes, find a source for professional tape duplicating. Work from the copies; keep the originals as archives. Label all tapes, noting whether they are originals or copies. If you are working with many tapes, create a log to keep track of the location and stage of each tape.

## 2. Create a Verbatim Transcript

Making a verbatim transcript means writing down every word, including broken sentences, false starts, and repetitions. Make decisions and choose options, such as whether to include nonverbal sounds—*um, er, uh-huhn*, [laughter], [phone rings], and so forth. These details all relate to the goal of the research and the purpose of the transcript.

Most people record a brief introductory statement about the purpose, date, and personnel of a tape-recorded event. If for some reason a recording does not include this information, create a statement at the beginning of the transcript that provides it.

Save a document of the initial transcript, noting the date and transcriptionist.

### 3. Review and Correct the Transcript against the Tape

When another person has transcribed your tape, compare the document on-screen or in hard copy with the tape and make corrections as needed. Reviewing, like copy editing, is demanding work. The fact is that reviewers may not hear or see discrepancies.

When I transcribe my own tapes, I build my review into the initial verbatim transcription. I listen to and type all the sections of a full sentence, then go back and listen again, perhaps three or four times, checking the sentence—or a longer segment—against the document on my computer screen. I make corrections and then listen and check one last time. I find that my ability to hear correctly and review accurately is far better at the time than reading a text against the tape later. This is my preference; it doesn't have to be yours.

You may have incorporated context and expressive information into the transcript already; if not, add context material following a review for corrections.

Save and print this version, noting the date and identifying the document as "Corrected verbatim transcript." This is the version to keep.

### 4. Where Relevant, Give Transcript to Others to Review

You may or may not need to have others review the transcript; this decision is specific to your work, project requirements, or contractual agreements with others. If you do need to have participants review the transcript, be forewarned that it involves additional time—often quite a lot.

If the transcript is being sent for review, participants may need to see a lightly edited version. Edit minimally for reading and comprehension. Editing is charged with implications—it alters the spoken word—but it is often a requirement of working with interviewees who may be unfamiliar with the sight of the spoken word. Save a copy of this version, noting the date and "First edit." You can send it to reviewers in hard copy or as an electronic file. Specify how you would like changes to be made—by hand on paper, in a computer document in a font of another color, or by some other means. You will undoubtedly have the ability to compare documents if reviewers make on-screen changes.

### 5. Make Changes if Necessary in Reviewed Transcript

When you have all necessary reviews of a transcript in hand, with corrections and changes, go over the changes. Keep all copies returned by reviewers with their changes. If reviewers edited on-screen, make sure the changes show in some way (through underlining, color highlighting, and so on) and, if you are keeping paper records, print this corrected version. Note the reviewer's name on each copy.

If necessary, check your agreements and your goals for the transcript to review whether you are bound to accept all changes. Make necessary corrections and minor edits that may be needed and proofread. Print out and save your corrected transcript, noting "Final version" and date.

### 6. Record Contextual Information; Index and Archive

If you have not already done so, add any necessary comments or context information (see chapter 4). Appendix A provides a form for this information, which includes names and thumbnail biographical sketches (include your own), event location, and date. Documentation is useful for your own later work, for publications, statements, and research protocols, for analysis, critique, history, and evaluation—even for legal purposes.

Save, print, and keep the final transcript, noting again the date and version. Send a copy to everyone who needs to receive one.

If an index to topics is necessary, create one (see chapter 5). Index the transcript by listing basic key topics relevant to your use and the pages on which they are found.

Archive the transcripts, tapes, and notes. Keep all tapes. Keep all versions of transcripts for the duration of the project. At some point you may want to cull, but it's a good idea to keep both the verbatim and final versions as well as reviewers' copies with changes.

## FORMATTING

At every stage in the preparation of the transcript, you will be faced with questions of formatting, both stylistic and technological. Giving some thought to these matters beforehand and having some guidelines in hand will make the job easier.

I take it for granted that transcripts will be created on a computer. Computers make the correction and editing of transcripts easier and faster.

Save all document versions for the duration of the research and always print out the corrected verbatim transcript and the final version. Keep these as records, noting the word processing program and version used, and date and label each version (do the same with any version you print out).

The basics of formatting a transcript are straightforward:

- Each speaker must be identified, by full name, initials, or last name, as you prefer (or, in some special cases, by pseudonym or other substitute). Each speaker's words should be started on a new line.
- Indicate where each side of each tape begins and ends: Tape 1: Side A; Tape 1: end Side A—Tape 1, Side B; Tape 1, end Side B—Tape 2: Side A, and so on.
- Number the pages.

Typically, transcripts are printed with double-spaced or one-and-a-half-spaced lines. Other common practices include the following:

- Numbering the lines. This is useful for quick reference and is essential if you are discussing, comparing, or analyzing transcripts in publications. If the transcript covers more than one tape, number the lines throughout the entire document (that is, the full written version of the taped event), not by individual tape. If you are numbering lines in a transcript that includes an original language with a line-by-line translation (see chapter 3), the original line and the translation get the same number, as follows:

  203   *Il entre, sans un mot; il ne me parle jamais.*
          He came in without a word; he never speaks to me.
  204   *Mais—*
          But—

- Noting the tape counter at different points, such as with each change of speaker or at each new page, paragraph, or section. This allows a reader to go to precisely that point in the tape to hear the passage. When using tape counters, roll the tape back to the very beginning of the tape (not just to the beginning of sound) before starting the tape counter and running the tape. Not all tape recorders have counters, but good professional models and transcribing machines will have them.

Give all the basic details of the event on the first page—date, names, place, and project. A running header consisting of a brief title or a name on each page may also be useful. If there are segments to the transcript—say, an interview that was recorded over several days—you might want to keep each section separate. You can either paginate the sections separately, change the date in the running header, or simply note on the first page the date of the new section (a table of contents will help in this case). In one interview that lasted three days, I paginated the whole interview sequentially but included the different dates in running heads.

There are a number of ways to present text so that it is readable:

- Indent all text of speech after the speaker's name so that names appear on the left, set off from all other text.
- Type names or initials in boldface. A word of caution here: italic type is used for specific purposes in a transcript, and you may want to reserve boldface to indicate something as well. For this reason, I advise selecting your type format for names (and context comments) after you know what form of notation, which includes typeface, you will need for the text.

## A BRIEF REVIEW OF STYLE GUIDES

Publication style guides, such as the *Chicago Manual of Style* and the *Publication Manual of the American Psychological Association*, can be useful. They deal with text and specifically with the publication of material that originates as written text. However, in translating from speech to written texts, use such guides sparingly and carefully. Be careful to let your notation system take priority and give publication conventions second place. In this book I have tried to use publication style manuals so that there is consistency between their suggested rules and the notations I suggest, especially for punctuation symbols. Transcription creates a text, but its origin lies in speech, and my advice and constant reminder is to try to retain this oral nature and not to make the spoken word appear (literally) too textual.

There are, however, many basic rules for which style manuals provide guidance. If you are publishing your transcripts, follow their rules about capitalization, the writing of numbers, names, terms, and places, and title terminology. Follow their usages for spelling, punctuation, and terminology (such as brand names and scientific, military, and religious terms). However, note that if speakers get a term wrong—such as a scientific name—you will have to consider the goals of your research before correcting it. You may need and they may want you to correct it, but there are situations in which correction of terms may be neither appropriate nor necessary. Also note that if a speaker expresses a false premise, you do not alter it.

The *Chicago Manual of Style*, 15th edition, pays attention to elements such as dialogue, distinctive treatment of words, and other features of writing that are found in literature rather than expository writing. Other style manuals focus precisely on academic publication (usually in specific disciplines) and on how to present text for both books and journal articles. Speakers— even academics—do not normally speak in the style of scientific publications, unless they are reading a paper at a conference (an instance that is often a good example of the difference between the written and the spoken word).

## VOICE RECOGNITION SOFTWARE

Voice recognition software has come a long way in the past few years and is invaluable in, for example, the medical and legal professions, where one person is recording his or her own voice for patient or client observations, memoranda, reports, and other kinds of office documents. Accuracy has improved, the program can be "taught," and punctuation can be included in the dictation. The rub, however, for social scientists or indeed anyone who records the voices of other people is that the software recognizes only one voice; it cannot handle two or more. Indeed, it is licensed for only one voice. Transcriptionists who work with several doctors or lawyers work with a separate software package for each professional. The solution, apparently used by many, is to listen to the tape recording and read what you hear into the microphone. Susan Tilley's article " 'Challenging' Research Practices: Turning a Critical Lens on the Work of Transcription" (2003) offers a good description of the use of such software for the kind of transcription discussed in this book.

Two software programs are, by all accounts, superior: Dragon Naturally Speaking and IBM ViaVoice. Dragon appears to be currently favored, as it has recently been improved and is said to be accurate "to between 95% and 98%." Reviews can be found in a variety of computer journals as well as on websites. Basic programs are not expensive—they run between $100 and $200. Special programs for the medical and legal professions, which include thesauri for technical terms, are far more expensive, almost $1,000, but clearly worth it. Digital recorders—again assuming that only one voice is involved—can also streamline the recording–transcribing–printing-out process, as the recording can be loaded directly into a computer, and the voice recognition software interfaces directly with it.

The benefit of using voice recognition programs is that some people prefer to spend time reading aloud rather than using a keyboard; the skill is simpler, and for these people the technology is faster. Many others prefer the technology whether or not it is faster. The drawback is that this rereading of original speech can produce many types of errors, especially if psychological elements of speech and other precise sounds are what you are trying to capture. The technology works best for interviews in which there are few speakers, content is the goal, and the recording is clear. You may find that this current technology provides no improvement in transcribing, either in time or final text; conversely, you may find that once you are accustomed to the program and to the precision you need in hearing and speaking, you can use it to produce a transcript in less time than you can using a keyboard.

If the original recording is of good quality, then the time required to produce a draft transcript using voice recognition software will be on the order of about three times the length of the recorded event. Roughly, this includes time to listen at least once to a short segment, repeat the words into the microphone or computer, and review that segment again. For a one-hour recording, then, you could produce a draft text in about three hours if you encountered no special challenges.

Once you have made the draft transcript, the review of the document (on-screen or in hard copy) against the original tape proceeds as normal. The voice recognition program permits corrections so that when you review the text against the tape, you can make on-screen corrections exactly as you would in traditional transcription and at the same stage.

The one problem with voice recognition software, as I see it, is that a third layer of interpretation—and possible error—is inserted into the scenario. Reviewing the draft transcript against the tape will, of course, help eliminate errors. Yet for some of the most challenging sorts of recordings—those of children, focus groups, and some kinds of performances—I really see few benefits and more problems. A good transcriptionist will be able to produce a better transcript that includes performance, psychological, and contextual aspects and probably can do it faster. It is not just keystroking time that is at issue; it is also skill and the ability to make decisions and gauge priorities. When working with several speakers whose speech overlaps, for example, you will need to decide where it is possible or impossible to extricate each speaker's words and where it might not be efficient to spend time doing so. The same applies to hard-to-understand speech such as that of children and elders and to poor-quality recordings (they occur). Here, voice recognition programs will add to time and effort rather than save it, and I believe the margin for errors would rise exponentially.

However, if most of your work consists of interviews for narration and content or if you are doing your own transcriptions, are used to this approach, and are a poor keyboard user, then reading your tape into voice recognition software may be an excellent solution. In this case, be exceptionally rigorous in reviewing the transcript against the tape.

# 3

# CREATING THE VERBATIM
# TRANSCRIPT

Transcripts begin with verbatim transcription in which every word the speaker said is written down. This is more complicated than it seems: people repeat words, start sentences and never finish them, play fast and loose with pronouns, and may—or may not—make them clearer through tone and emphasis. And that does not even begin to cover the nonverbal elements of communication. Speakers use nonwords frequently; their pauses, gestures, and facial expressions contribute to meaning, as do objects in their immediate environment. How is this to be translated into writing?

Making a verbatim transcript requires skill in hearing and understanding what is being said and in using conventions of the printed word—spelling, punctuation, and sentence structure—so that speech makes sense in writing. In this chapter, I discuss the elements of speech and communication that are of particular concern in ethnographic transcription. I follow the principles that transcription should be consistent, acknowledging that specialist needs, particularly those of linguists, will require special notations. Rather than each transcriber creating a new set of notations, notations should start simply and build up to the desired level of specificity, never reusing symbols that already have a function. The discussion is not exhaustive; rather, my aim is to present a basic set of notations, drawing on conventional practices—that is, practices common in publishing in North America—for use by people who are not linguists, who create texts using ethnographic methods in order to analyze the spoken word for other than linguistic purposes, and who may want to make their transcripts accessible to generalists.

Dennis Tedlock, an anthropologist who explores languages and their grammatical elements as well as storytelling, poetry, and the expressive nature of the spoken word, notes in his book *The Spoken Word and the Work of Interpretation* (1983) that no transcript can re-create a tape. He comments that notation should "follow a path between the conventions handed down in literate tradition and the purely hypothetical goal of total notation. Considered practically, notation should not be so complex as to slow the eye of the sight-reader" (p. 6). This point is crucial for all transcription.

Researchers who create transcripts for their own use can, of course, follow any notation system that seems useful. But creating individualistic notation sets is not ideal because research papers and data are rarely confined to one person. Students and other researchers may share them, as may participants in the recorded event. Anything may end up in an archive. And, of course, researchers who publish even short segments of transcripts need to ensure that their readers will understand their notations. Authors who use specific notations often provide a key to them in publications, and this is an excellent idea. Others rely on a certain visual presentation that seems transparent: capital letters, for example, to indicate loud speech. Specialists generally write for a readership that shares their notation conventions, but they, too, often include keys to their systems. This sort of creativity in fact builds from a fairly standard, shared system; it is only the more complex elements of talk that receive special (and usually inconsistent) symbols. I believe it is time to bring recognition to this standard system and firm up a few details.

## THE IMPLICATIONS OF EDITING

Before tackling verbatim transcription, I want to address editing. Though most of us think of editing as changes made to a draft of a written text, for readability, editing really consists of two separate activities. The first is the act of transcribing itself, in which you use the conventions of writing— spelling, punctuation, paragraph divisions, and the distinguishing of words from nonwords—to represent the spoken word. Simply representing words in standard spelling already "edits" our speech. The second kind of editing is that in which you alter the verbatim transcript by cutting words, smoothing out—to a greater or lesser extent—the oral qualities of a written text. You may indeed want to edit your verbatim transcript that way later on; whether, when, and how to do it makes up much of the subject matter of chapter 4. The sea change from spoken to written starts with the way in which we write our language down. Editing has implications, and we need to recognize them before beginning to transcribe.

Speech needs to be transferred into a form that matches your analytical needs. In a lightly edited verbatim transcript, the words are changed as little as possible; this is the version I prefer. But for some purposes you may want to turn the spoken word into a more easily read text—that is, into a written document rather than one that tries to capture the nature of speech. Oral historians do this, co-constructing a written document with the active participation of the interviewee. Ethnographers, too, co-construct dialogue, but in most ethnographic endeavors it is an oral construction. Ethnographers are more interested in a contextualized play of words, actions, and interactions between players than are oral historians.

Editing alters the spoken word. Of course, transcription does this no matter what degree of editing is applied. Employing the conventions of writing is essential and, like any other kind of translation, can be done well. The more the words of a transcript are changed, however, the more the spoken word is altered. Although the language in a transcript has already ceased to be "spoken," it is worth asking, What further reshaping is appropriate, and for what end? When a passage is unclear, for example, editing can help bring out its meaning—as you understand it. It can formalize grammar so that the speaker's meaning, which might have been conveyed through gestures or context during the original event, is "correct." This meaning may be exactly as the speaker intended it, but it may not.

If your concern is speech, exactly as spoken, and if your analysis relies on such precision, then the only editing you should do, both as you transcribe and later, is to use the conventions of writing well and consistently, adding any comments or contextual information you think necessary. Transcripts are created for reading, analysis, and ease of access. If you edit as you go, do so carefully, taking into full consideration the implications of every change and alteration.

## WHAT "EVERY WORD" IMPLIES

Transcribing begins with a verbatim transcription. What does it mean to transcribe "every word"? Let me illustrate this with an example from one of my interviews:

> They never lost a thing there, and then the ceremonial built that grand-stand there, and they moved a lot of that, and then later they tore down the hogans and moved to this modern garbage that's over there now. And those records were moved over to underneath the grandstand, there was a steel grandstand, and there was some nasty storage areas. But a water leak came in and it did destroy some things, not everything but a few things, and whatever that may be. But then M___ came in and—and record keeping, it was throwing somewhere. He did that with art works,

there was [*inaudible word*] like Alan [?Houser] paintings, throws it up on top of a book case you can't reach, then throws a bunch of garbage on top of it. And he just did not do real well.

This is a verbatim quote. The punctuation includes commas, inserted either where I heard minimal pauses or for ease of reading, em dashes where there was a repetition, and periods where sentences ended or where it seemed to me that they ended. I used capital letters (and, in the full text, paragraphs). I left in false starts, did not tidy up grammar, and changed no words. I have used underscores to indicate a name I purposely omitted and noted a word I could not hear and a word I guessed from context and knowledge of the name, placing both items in square brackets. The creative action of transcribing is to know what to include, whether to leave anything out, and how to indicate what you are doing.

In order to make such decisions, it is important first to review the goals of your transcription. Why are you making a transcript, and for what purpose? The answer to this question is key to all your decisions in creating a written text. I want to repeat an important point here: neither audio-nor videotapes represent the full reality, any more than a transcript will. Audiotapes capture only sounds. Videotapes can capture other important aspects, such as movement, gestures, and expressions. Notes are important to provide some frameworks such as speakers' identities and contexts that are relevant to the research. But all representations are a form of shorthand, a necessary reduction in the river of information that we inhabit naturally as communicators. Decide what is important for your transcript—what "every word" means for you—on the basis of your research and your goals for analysis or readership.

Transcribing every word does not necessarily mean transcribing a recording in its entirety. Sometimes, making a partial transcript can be useful, either to refer to or to quote. I once made a transcription that consisted of three sentences, a tiny part of a much longer recording. In making a partial transcription, be aware of the dangers of decontextualizing material or of making it seriously misleading. Be sure to capture full sentences and include material at the beginning and the end that may not be relevant but will be useful to show how the topic arose in the midst of another discussion. Use the same methods you would for a full transcript and provide the same kinds of contextual information about date, speakers, and place and perhaps even a brief comment about the major direction of the speech. Note the tape's title and/or number and its date. It's useful also to give the tape counter for the beginning and end of the segment you are transcribing so that you or others can find the segment on the full tape.

# FROM SOUND TO TEXT: THE CONVENTIONS
# OF WRITING

You have made a copy tape to use for transcribing, you have decided on a visual format, and you have a transcriptionist—yourself or someone else. Now to begin the transcription. As you listen to the recording and type the words, you will automatically rely on the conventions of writing. But there are many to choose from. In the rest of this chapter, I list some typical elements of speaking, discuss whether to represent or exclude each in a transcript, and recommend notations to be used.

## *Speech and Spelling*

Over thousands of years, spoken language has been turned into conventional written forms with standardized spellings that do not always represent its sound phonetically. In every language, conventional spelling plays havoc with the way we say a word, reflecting history in the very orthography we use. Many words in English are spelled oddly in comparison with the way they are pronounced: *rough, know*. Other words are commonly mispronounced in ways that don't reflect their spelling—*nucular* (nuclear), *mischeevious* (mischievous)—the list is long. We are used to it. Indeed, so used are we to conventional spelling that writing words in a transcript as they are pronounced tends to slow down our reading. We need to examine why we want to use nonstandard spellings to reproduce pronunciation in a transcript—the tape is a better source.

Variety in pronunciation reflects culture, social structure, and region. Sometimes representing exact pronunciation in spelling ("eye dialect," as Edward Ives calls it) is necessary to one's research goals, but if this is not the case in your work, then you should use standard spelling; reproducing pronunciations can seem patronizing. (For a strong statement against using "eye dialect," see Ives 1995:81.) In literature, nonstandard spelling is often used to represent variety of pronunciation. In transcripts it can produce curious and inconsistent representations of words. Here is a sentence from a published transcript that wanted to capture sounds:

> he's gotta temper anyway, he js::: wa:::::::h screamed iz damn e:ngine yihknow [Schegloff 1992:217].

At least two words here—*screamed* and *e:ngine*—retain "normal" spellings (colons represent prolonged vowels), even though they don't reflect pronunciation phonetically at all, whereas other spellings try to indicate how the words were pronounced. One word—*yihknow*—is an odd hybrid, combining the linguistically precise "yih" (you) with the traditionally spelled "know." *Y'know* would have been fine, less precise phonetically, but then so is "know." The combination of standard spelling and phonetic spelling is not entirely obvious to the nonlinguistic reader.

There *are* occasions that call for the use of transcribed dialect or pronunciation; you will determine these according to your research needs. One means for handling such transcriptions is the International Phonetic Alphabet (IPA), developed by linguists to reproduce the sounds of speech in writing. Using it requires familiarity with phonetics and skill in both transcription and analysis. The IPA is useful, however, when you need to pinpoint the pronunciation of one or a few words, which can be given brackets after the standard orthographic version.

On the other hand, there are many words whose colloquial flavor and nonstandard spelling have crept into writing. And some contractions, of course, are considered standard English and appear in dictionaries (*aren't, can't, don't, won't*); these should be transcribed as speakers say them. Others are colloquial (*wanna, y'know*) and even officially ungrammatical, that is, in writing (*ain't*). Many other words have common colloquial forms, such as the varieties of *yes* that we all produce in speech: *yeah, yup, mm-hmm,* and so forth. How should you represent these in your transcript? And does it matter?

I think that the art of transcription lies in knowing when to capture colloquial words and when to ignore variant pronunciations—the distinction is sometimes quite subtle. Contrary to my general advice about not trying to transcribe dialects and variant pronunciations, I think that commonly spoken words such as *yeah* and *ain't* should be included in transcripts if they are the words the speaker indeed used. On the other hand, *wanna* and *gonna be* (pronounced by most of us some of the time) should not be used. If you include colloquialisms, listen to the speaker and transcribe the words he or she says using the most easily recognized spelling possible. Unless you are specifically trying to reproduce the sounds of spoken language, the details of variant pronunciations are best heard in your original tape recording, not represented in your transcript.

Sometimes people create words or use special or local terms for which the dictionary is unhelpful. Spell them out as you hear them. Never use [*sic*]. In publishing, it is used to point up a word in a quotation that either is erroneous or could be understood to be an error in the original. In transcripts, the speech of participants is what it is—correct as produced. Your opinion of it (as opposed to your analysis), as indicated by the patronizing *sic* in the transcript, is irrelevant. Readers will assume the transcription is accurate, and your methods will ensure it.

## Punctuation

After spelling, the most important decisions you will make about how to transcribe "every word" are those concerning punctuation. The basic function of punctuation, a system of symbols developed over time that writing and publishing themselves developed, is to ease comprehension in reading. Lacking sound, expression, and similar sorts of contextual pointers used in oral communication, writing needs other aids. Punctuation helps break the flow of words, and it works with grammar to clarify what the words are intended to mean.

There are two camps in the use of punctuation in transcription. One uses virtually no punctuation except periods, sometimes dashes, and sometimes the spacing of lines on the page to convey pauses (see Ellen Basso 1985). In the other camp, punctuation is used (but not overused) to reflect something of the phrasing and spacing of oral speech. I belong to this second camp.

Because punctuation is not always evident in oral speech, adding it may insert interpretation. Use it with care. I apply punctuation for ease of reading and comprehension. I take it for granted that I influence the transcript in many ways, and I feel punctuation is the least intrusion I make. Here is an example from a transcript that I have stripped of punctuation, except for a period placed where the speaker stopped. The three dots indicate where I have cut out words—here, plant names:

> And what I did was that I planted trees on the reclamation area and I did a lot of did a lot of reclaiming and just kind of overseeing the end of the just labor just plain old labor you know made fence when it was all done being mined we made a lot of fence we did a lot of land we planted everything that you could ever think of sagebrush to just plain old weed [ . . . ] everything that anything that you would see out here they planted over there and that's what we had to plant in our areas and then they had to make those after they had done mining they had to try to build it back up to the natural way so we were the last ones to leave from that area.

In transcribing word for word, you need not be a grammatician to use basic punctuation—commas, periods, and dashes. You, the transcriptionist, listening to the recording, can hear the pauses and intonations that indicate sentences or phrases and can put in what might be described as "natural punctuation." Here is the same excerpt as I punctuated it in the transcript.

I used the speaker's pauses and intonations as a guide:

> And what I did was that I planted trees on the reclamation area, and I did
> a lot of—did a lot of reclaiming, and just kind of overseeing the end of
> the—just labor, just plain old labor. You know, made fence when it was
> all done being mined, we made a lot of fence. We did a lot of land, we
> planted everything that you could ever think of—sagebrush, to just plain
> old weed [ . . . ]—anything that you would see out here, they planted over
> there. And that's what we had to plant in our areas. And then they had to
> make those, after they had done mining, they had to try to build it back
> up to the natural way. So we were the last ones to leave from that area.

The three major notations I recommend using are commas, periods,
and dashes. Commas indicate very slight pauses, breaks between segments of a
sentence. Periods mark the ends of sentences. Dashes punctuate incomplete
sentences. Here we encounter the first conflict between the oral and the
written. Not everyone speaks in complete sentences—that is, utterances that
involve a subject and a verb—and almost no one speaks in full sentences all
the time. Everyone—you, me, and well-paid invited speakers—will at one
point or another use incomplete sentences. There is nothing wrong with
this; incomplete sentences are fluent aspects of the spoken word and are
often stylistically powerful. Most of the time we can understand them. Even
in writing, incomplete sentences can be stylistically appropriate.

Dashes are necessary in transcripts. This is the best punctuation not just
for unfinished sentences but also for sentences that are started several times
(false starts) and for repetitions of words and phrases, all so common in speech.
I want to mention ellipsis points here, too. In publication they are always
used, without brackets, to indicate material that has been cut; in addition, the
*Chicago Manual of Style* suggests their use in "faltering speech." In transcripts,
they are frequently used to indicate incomplete phrases, pauses, or hesitation,
used wherever I suggest placing an em dash. So frequently have ellipses been
so used, in fact, that I believe that some stronger indication needs to be
given for their use to indicate cut material. I recommend (as you will see)
that ellipsis points used to indicate cut material be placed in square brackets.

Semicolons and colons are, in my view, unnecessary, especially because
they begin to create a subtle change to a more literary style of writing.
Parentheses could be used to indicate a speaker's parenthetical remarks, but
they are not necessary. A remark may clearly be an aside or a digression from
the main topic, and no punctuation is needed to indicate this. In transcripts,
parentheses are better kept for other purposes. If you think they would help
make a remark less confusing, then use them, but you could achieve this also
by breaking the speech into paragraphs at the point of digression.

Exclamation points are useful to point up irony or humor, though again they should be used carefully, for it is not always clear to readers what they signal in a transcript. Laughter is best noted as [laughter]. Exclamation points can be helpful to indicate a joke when the humor was evident in the speaker's voice or face, which the interviewer sees but another transcriber cannot. Interpretation and the researcher's goals will be important in deciding whether and where to use exclamation points.

In general, I strongly recommend using standard punctuation symbols for their conventional (published) meanings. Publication style manuals can be useful guides to conventional symbols (see chapter 2). But because a transcript is not a typical text or manuscript, conventional usage is rarely sufficient, and thus style guides will not help in all aspects of transcribing the spoken word. The accepted use is only a starting point. In appendix B, I list the conventional punctuation symbols and give their standard uses (in publications), some notes on the variety of uses to which symbols have been put in transcriptions, and the uses I recommend for transcriptions.

## False Starts, Unfinished Sentences, and Faltering Speech

Speech is not always—or often—produced in full sentences. Speakers frequently start, stop, and start again. They repeat themselves. They begin thoughts and sentences and do not finish them. Sometimes all this is evident in pauses between broken phrases or incomplete sentences, but sometimes it is not evident at all until you read the text.

In a full, word-for-word text, transcribe all false starts, partial sentences, and repeated words or phrases, using em dashes between them. Meaning may be left hanging, right along with the sentence, as it is in this example:

> I started—started to run—run towards the group. I think I ran all the way. But I—when I got abreast of them, I stopped. I don't know—. When I got there, I saw what they were looking at.

The partial sentence "I don't know" has been punctuated with a dash and the next phrase treated as the beginning of a sentence. (It could also have been punctuated as "I don't know—when I got there, I saw what they were looking at.") The first phrase has no particular meaning, but it could be psychological evidence or could be serving to build suspense in the narrative.

Incomplete sentences might better be seen as completed phrases that do not match grammatical writing, usually because they lack a verb. People speak in incomplete sentences all the time. Sometimes these are expressive and comprehensible; sometimes they are not. Usually they will be more or less comprehensible—perhaps by inflection or manner of expression.

Occasionally, especially in writing, incomplete sentences may allow more than one interpretation. The difference between an incomplete sentence and a false start or broken and repeated phrase is subtle; intonation is key. Transcribe an incomplete sentence as it is spoken and punctuate it using periods.

Faltering speech is what you hear when a speaker's voice trails away, leaving a sentence unfinished. Representations of faltering speech may be more appropriate for literature than for transcription, but your research will help you define what is relevant and when faltering speech is, in fact, taking place and should be noted. If you can distinguish faltering, hesitant speech from very slow or thoughtful speech, this has often been done by means of ellipsis points:

> GB: I don't know how I felt. I didn't think about it. I just . . . I just . . .
> Interviewer: Yes?

But pauses or repetitions so often occur with faltering speech that in my view it is better, and equally appropriate, to transcribe the previous text with dashes but to also include the speakers' pauses to make clearer their hesitant speech:

> GB: I don't know how I felt. I didn't think about it. I just—I just—
> [pause]
> Interviewer: Yes?

On the whole, I recommend dashes rather than ellipsis points. Not only is it a common use, it avoids conflicting use of ellipsis points for both cut material and faltering speech. However, I still recommend indicating cuts by placing ellipsis points in brackets to make it absolutely clear.

Stammering and stuttering are other kinds of speech that should, when relevant, be noted. Stammering is a shorter form of repetition: I—I—well, I don't know. Use em dashes, as indicated previously for word repetition. In novels, it's used often with consonants: w-w-well? But that is not exactly how people speak. If someone does exactly that, use a hyphen. Stuttering, however, is very different. Here, if it is necessary, use a hyphen; but I expect that there are people who study stuttering and, if creating a transcript, will need and devise a specific notation.

### Filler Words and Nonverbal Sounds

Should the transcript include such things as filler words, nonwords, and other sounds, especially laughter and weeping? Fillers may be stylistic, nonwords have meanings, and other sounds are often highly relevant to the emotion or tone of the recorded event. They deserve to be transcribed. Contrarily, some people have habits such as clearing their throats that accompany every utterance and are essentially meaningless nonverbal acts; others may simply have a cold. Such nonverbal elements should not be transcribed.

## FILLERS

Fillers, also called tag words, are words or phrases that people insert into their speech over and over again, almost unconsciously. "You know" is one of them, along with "so," "like" (and "like, you know"), "and then," and so on. Many people start every sentence with "and" or "but." Such fillers perform a very minor function, more like a pause or a nonverbal expression.

In a verbatim transcript, filler words should all be included. However, fillers can be irritating to read, and you may decide to edit them out later—or even at the verbatim transcribing stage, despite my recommendations. Often, if participants review transcripts, they will automatically edit them out. I discuss this issue further in chapter 4.

## ASSENT AND DISSENT SOUNDS

Sounds of assent, spelled variously (*uh-huh, mm-hmm*), and dissent (*uh-uh, uhn-uhn*) should be included in your verbatim transcript. These can have a verbal meaning, though some play a role somewhat like fillers. Often they indicate that the speaker is listening. Decide how these sounds are to be spelled and be consistent throughout. You might also note, when relevant, [agrees] and [disagrees] for clarity.

Often, people (especially interviewers) make sounds of assent or dissent at the same time others are speaking. Overlapping assents, especially on the part of the interviewer, who may be showing interest or attention, may be cut unless the full interaction needs to be presented in the transcript for analysis. I discuss the convention for writing simultaneous speech later.

## OTHER NONVERBAL SOUNDS

These include *um, er*, grunts (all of which are less clearly assent or dissent), throat clearings, and small coughs or sighs before speaking. *Um* and *er* are often included in verbatim transcripts, but grunts and other such sounds usually are not. If they are not critical to your research, you have the option of including them at the verbatim stage and editing them out later or not including them at all. Leave them in if absolute verbatim precision is essential for your research goal. Diagnostic interviews, especially, may focus on such sounds. *Um*, for example, especially in mid-sentence, might indicate either hesitation or uncertainty. Coughs can be strategic. Again, consider the usefulness of the original recording as opposed to the transcript here.


## LAUGHTER

Laughter is usually entered in a transcript as a context note in square brackets: [laughs], if one person is laughing, and [laughter], if more than one person laughs. In some disciplines, laughter is timed: [laughter 3 seconds].

In some cases people laugh not so much because something is funny as because it is a sound they make at the end of every section of speech. It appears to function in rather the same way as other nonwords. Should these sorts of laughs be transcribed? Including them in the first verbatim draft may allow you to avoid interpreting them too soon; later you can decide whether to edit them out.

Many humorous remarks are not accompanied by laughter but are communicated by tone of voice or context. In these cases, exclamation points are useful. The *Chicago Manual of Style* notes that exclamation points should be used to mark "an outcry or an emphatic or ironic comment." Indicate humor and irony, a slightly different form of humor, by the sparing use of exclamation points. Humor and irony are cultural and can be hard to grasp—I have had the uncomfortable experience, more than once, of making an ironic comment that was taken at face value. If you are uncertain, either leave the expression unmarked or make a comment such as [speaker may intend a joke] or [?humor] or even [I could not tell whether this was a joke or not]. When appropriate, you might include a context comment such as [*name* laughs throughout].


## WEEPING

Weeping is sometimes hard to discern on a tape. Tears are inaudible; only the interviewer will know if the speaker cries silently. The interviewee might even try to keep emotion hidden—not everyone wears his heart on his sleeve. And exactly how should a transcriber indicate the breaking voice of someone recounting a tragedy? How might such an emotional moment be described with both accuracy and delicacy? Journalists are fond of keeping the microphone running for just such telling (or intrusive) moments; what should the transcriber do? Here, noting pauses or writing a contextual comment in square brackets should be helpful, especially if emotion interrupts speech and lasts a little while. You can note a tone of voice, such as [with sadness], or indicate [tears] or [blows nose]. The goal of the interview and your relations with reviewers of the transcript will help you know how to include weeping.

### Pauses

Pauses are an integral part of natural speech. A very brief pause may indicate sentence structure and call for representation with a comma. Sometimes a brief pause occurs in a series of repetitions, a broken sentence, or a false start and is best represented by a dash. It is worth paying attention to the typical spacing of each speaker's words; some speakers simply talk more slowly and pause more than others, and their doing so reveals nothing about meaning. A prolonged pause is a silence and might even be a particular kind of response—to a question, for instance.

The goals of your research will dictate whether you note pauses in your verbatim transcript. If you do not need them or if you feel they are not meaningful to a specific speaker, leave them out. If a particular pause seems to you to be meaningful, include it. If you do include them, ask yourself when they should be indicated by a comma or a dash or mentioned as [pause].

In my own interviews, speakers rarely pause for long, and I use commas or dashes to indicate the natural spacing of their speech. If they stop to think, I may or may not note the pause; it is usually not relevant to my research. But in many other tape recordings I have heard and transcripts I have read, pauses are important.

In certain types of recordings, such as interviews for psychological analysis, pauses are timed. If you want to time pauses, indicate the time in seconds in square brackets. This can be done in any of several ways: [pause 1 sec.], [1 sec.], or merely [1.0]. If you get silence or a long pause and you are not timing pauses, you might want to note it: [does not answer question] or [long pause]. Or you might want to time that particular pause: [*name* is silent for 20 seconds]. If you time a pause when you do not usually do so, it will be because you believe that pause to be significant, so think carefully about why you are interpreting it that way.

### Overlapping Speech

When two or more people speak at the same time, their words are typically represented in transcripts by the use of parentheses or brackets. There are three types: parentheses ( ), square brackets [ ], and curly or flourished brackets (also known as braces) { }. I prefer curly brackets, a typographic symbol now available to anyone with a computer, because it has no other use in transcription. Published transcripts use any of the three, and often the symbol is elongated so that it brackets the overlapped portions, beginning and end, in one typological mark.

Place a curly bracket at the point where joint speech begins and another where it ends. Often, overlapping speech is spaced on the lines of the page so that the overlapping portions start together. If you can hear who is saying what, give the speaker's name. Here is a basic representation of overlapping speech:

> MJ:     I found the story in a book. But it was different—and I can't
>         remember where I put it. {Would somebody find it?}
> DDJ:                            {I know where it is.}
> MJ:     I'd really like to read it {again}.
> DDJ:                            {Here}.

Often, a speaker will make an assent sound that interrupts or overlaps dialogue. Many transcripts show this as an insert in parentheses, with the name or initials of the speaker, within the main speaker's words:

> Allen: I had the weirdest feeling that I was being followed
> (Mary: uh-huh), and it scared me.

It could also be separated out using curly brackets:

> Allen: I had the weirdest feeling that I was being {followed}
> Mary:                                            {uh-huh}
> Allen: and it scared me.

The benefit of the first method is simplicity. If the dialogue breaks off and another speaker makes an assent sound—that is, the words are not spoken at the same time—then showing this on separate lines (as above, but without the brackets) would be appropriate.

*Reported Speech*

When speaking, people often report the speech of others. They do this either directly, as a quotation:

> He told me, I never said that.

or indirectly:

> He told me that he had never said that.

Indirect speech can either be placed in quotation marks or simply separated by commas, as I did in the first example here. This is the way I usually handle reported speech, for a somewhat pedantic reason: the speaker probably is not quoting precisely but merely giving her version of a speech. Publishing style guides give both methods; the choice is up to you.

*Inaudible or Incomprehensible Words on Tape*

Despite taking every care to have a clear recording, there will be times when you or another transcriptionist cannot understand a word or phrase that a speaker is saying. If you cannot hear or understand part of the tape, even after multiple listenings, there are several ways to note the fact, all of them in square brackets: [   ] (a blank space; this is least clear); [——] (a two-em dash, which also indicates an intentional omission, usually a name or some other word, to protect privacy or other information); [inaudible word(s)] or [words unclear]. I prefer [inaudible words], as it is perfectly clear. If possible, try to give the number of missing words: [inaudible 3+ words]. If you cannot even distinguish the number of words, just put [inaudible words].

If you make a guess or insert probable words, put this in square brackets preceded by a question mark: [?love of my life]. If you are working with a transcriptionist, you may want to make sure that he does not write [garbled] or [nonsense]. The words may sound garbled to him, but the speaker undoubtedly did not garble his words or utter nonsense. It is the listener who simply cannot hear what was said.

*Paragraphs*

As writers we learn to break topics into paragraphs. This is not always the case in speech, but speakers almost always pause naturally before starting a new flow of ideas. Even if they don't pause, they often speak in content-oriented chunks. Written texts use paragraphs to organize the contents into segments focused on a particular topic as well as to break up a block of text on a page. I recommend using paragraphs to break speech, either by content or after a pause. This can be done while making the verbatim transcription or later, during review and editing.

Since speakers are also simultaneously thinking on their feet, they may insert comments, or "flashbacks"—remarks related to earlier questions or topics. The decision whether to begin a new paragraph for such remarks or to leave them embedded in the surrounding content, as they were in speech, is one you will make based on your analytic needs.

If you have recorded two or more speakers, each speaker provides the break point for a "paragraph." But one speaker might talk for several minutes, creating, in the transcript, a great block of text. Although this is not really problematic, paragraphs are helpful to readers and analysts. Again, you might use the speaker's pauses to create paragraphs in his or her segment of speech. And note that you can end a paragraph with a dash if the spoken words warrant one.

*Volume, Emphasis, and Other Expressive Devices*

Speakers create expressive effects through emphasis, tone, pitch, prolongation of sound, and volume. There are times when it is critical to include such effects in a transcript and times when it is not. Different people have published transcripts that include various expressive notations. Emphasis is often useful or necessary. Transcriptions of performance in particular need to attend to many aspects of speech and action. Poetry, too, is challenging; breaks in line can represent breathing points and pauses, and this in turn implies meaning. For more on performance and poetry, see chapter 4.

VOLUME

People have represented volume in any of several ways. One transcription showed increasing loudness by placing different symbols over loud, louder, and loudest words. Most often, loud speech is represented by writing words in all capital letters—"I will not say it ONE MORE TIME"—and this is the method I recommend. Soft speech has been shown by a textual comment—[softly]—by the use of smaller letters and by symbols placed over the softer words. I recommend either using smaller print or adding a textual comment such as [quietly] in square brackets to denote lower volume.

## EMPHASIS

Emphasis is usually shown by either italics or underlining. Both seem equally clear, but my recommendation is to use underlining (see also appendix B). The reason for this is that italics have other standard, consistent uses, as I will discuss; both italics and underlining can be used together and may be needed to show simultaneous features (such as emphasis in a second language).

Both italics and underlining have several usages in transcripts. Italics are always used to indicate words in another language, especially in transcripts with simultaneous translation. Many transcripts use italics for all context comments, a practice that usefully sets off such additions. (Context comments should always appear within square brackets, whether or not they are also italicized.) Underlining is used in some transcripts to show rising pitch.

Another way of emphasizing words in speech is to pronounce them with prolonged vowels or consonants. Such pronunciations can be represented by any of three methods: repeated letters (meeeeee), a four-em dash (do----wn) (both in Tedlock 1982:000), and colons (me:::, do:::::wn). The argument for a four-em dash is that repeating a letter can be confusing, perhaps making the word look as if the pronunciation is changing (doooooown). Here, there is some choice. Repeating the letter usually works well, I think, though it does run some risk of altering pronunciation; both a colon and four-em dashes work equally well. Both may be obvious, but in some places the transcript may need a key for clarity.

## TONE, INTONATION, AND PITCH

Speakers show a great range of tones of voice and intonation and other expressive devices to add to meaning and performance. These elements of speech fall in the area of specialists who should be the ones to develop notation. Here, I suggest only adding comments such as [angry], [pleased], [sing-song], [flat voice], when you can be certain of interpretation, to indicate them. This is not ideal because it can lead toward overinterpretation, so use such comments carefully.

Changes in pitch, too, require special notation. They have been shown in various ways: by raising the type increasingly higher or by increasingly lowering it (Tedlock 1982); by adding context comments such as [high], [higher], [low], and [slight rise]; and sometimes by underlining the high- or low-pitched words. I have also seen accent marks (´) placed on the highest-pitched word. If pitch is important and if raising or lowering the type on the page is problematic, then context comments or accent marks are useful.

Some discourse analysts, linguists, and other scholars need to mark tone, pitch, volume, falling or rising voice, and lengthened segments of words simultaneously. They use an array of symbols to indicate these elements, such as arrows over words, degree symbols, question marks, and slashes (for an example, see appendix C; also, examine some of the fuller transcripts in Duranti and Goodwin 1992). Transcripts that indicate tone are not easy for generalists to read, but I think this is the nature of specialist notation. People who use extensive markings need them and usually provide a key. I suggest that such extended notations avoid symbols that have conventional usages in transcriptions, such as those I have described here.

## TRANSCRIBING AND TRANSLATING
## FOREIGN LANGUAGES

This book is geared toward transcripts made in the language of the recorder and transcriptionist or in a language the researcher speaks fluently. Yet other languages often appear in speech. In some of my recorded interviews, for example, Navajo words crop up. Many people switch easily from one language to another, "code-switching" into languages the recorder or transcriptionist may not know. Occasionally speakers use a few words in another language they do not know well and perhaps mispronounce.

There are several ways to handle recorded speech that includes other languages. If you are doing your own transcription and are reasonably familiar with the other language, listen carefully and try to write down exactly what you hear. If the language is a written one, check a dictionary for accuracy and spelling. If the language is an unwritten or rarely written one and you are familiar with it, you will know the best way to transliterate it or to locate someone who can. If you are unfamiliar with the language, it will be helpful to locate a fluent speaker. You might be able to enlist the help of the recorded speaker, depending on whether she is used to writing her own language. A linguist from a nearby university might be helpful, either one who knows the language or one who can help you identify sounds and transliterate them using either standard orthography or the phonetic alphabet.

If you are using a transcriptionist who is unfamiliar with any of the languages appearing on the tape, ask him or her not to transliterate any of those words but to indicate the omitted section in square brackets [*words in (name the language)*] wherever they appear. It's also useful to have the transcriptionist note the tape counter at that point and perhaps to indicate whether the section is one or a few words or longer. You can then fill in the blanks when you check the transcription against the tape. This procedure will save time and prevent errors because it is difficult for a transcriptionist to accurately hear the sounds produced in an unfamiliar language.

If the speaker uses only a few words in another language or if they code-switch—switch between two languages—you may be able to transcribe them yourself. If there is considerable dialogue, you may need a translator or a linguist who can write the language. Languages vary in the degree to which they can be transliterated into the English alphabet or need special symbols for special sounds. Use italics for all words in another language.

Linguists and others who specialize in the spoken word are well versed in the IPA. For a couple of sources, see Victoria Fromkin's *Linguistics* (2000) or look up the International Phonetic Alphabet on the Internet. (Each volume of the *Handbook of North American Indians* also provides a simplified version of this alphabet with English equivalents, listed as Technical Alphabet in the tables of contents.) It is easy enough to obtain the font (it does not come with most computers). If you do want to use it, you should consider whether your readers are familiar with it; if not, it is a good idea to include as an appendix the relevant symbols you are using.

Transliteration is not easy, even for those who speak a language that has not typically been written. For example, Navajo is now a written language, with a dictionary, grammars, publications, and textbooks. Many announcements, reports, and newsletters in the Navajo Nation are printed in Navajo, and a Navajo word-processing program has recently been produced. But not every speaker automatically knows how to write or spell all the words. When I transcribe it, I look up the words in a comprehensive Navajo dictionary, helped by a translation by the speaker into English. When I cannot find all the words I hear on tape, I transliterate as best I can using standard Navajo orthography with its special letters.

Translation is another topic. When a whole speech is translated, the two texts should appear together, either line by line or side by side in columns, one in italic the other in roman typeface. Sometimes a translation is made quite literally, according to the meaning of morphemes rather than the way the words would actually be said in the second language. In such cases, the text is presented line by line, with the original words above and the translation below (an example is shown in appendix C). Such texts are translations for precision of speech, not for colloquiality or literary quality. Often, literal translations are accompanied by a third translation for sense.

There are many ways in which people handle translation in oral history. One superb oral historian whose work I saw was writing his native Yup'ik on the left-hand side of a page and an English translation, matched sentence for sentence, on the right. The English was fluent, sometimes incorporating colloquial modern expressions and sometimes translating Yup'ik literally. It was often much longer than the Yup'ik version because single words for which there was no precise equivalent had to be turned into phrases. The transcript was an example of bilingual fluency and excellent methods.

In another example, a Cheyenne colleague worked on a series of interviews in her community. She taped them in the Cheyenne language and translated them into English for the transcript. This translation, too, was colloquial and modern. She did not create a written text in Cheyenne; everyone agreed that the tape provided the best "text" for Cheyenne speech and would be far more useful for people who wanted to preserve and teach the language. The tapes provide a source for pronunciation and the voices of elders with all their expressive tones.

Translation always poses some kind of problem. Most concepts manage to scramble over the boundaries between languages, but some make it only with difficulty and not without a few scratches and bruises. Puns and wordplay are lost, shading may not be understood, and cultural context may seem mystifying. But it can be done, and it should be—loss of some kind is acceptable if there is a gain in broader knowledge of the world. We all know of books that have enriched us even in translation. If you are not doing your own translation, then try to find the best translator for the language spoken, and make sure he or she is able handle the dialect or style of the region or social group to which the speaker belongs. Play a section of the tape for possible translators and ask whether they can pinpoint the region or dialect, noting their reactions and first attempts.

When you include translations in your transcript, either discuss it in the opening information or, in the case of short passages, type the original word, phrase, or sentence in italics and place the translation after it in square brackets. If an entire transcript is a translation, decide how to present it. Ideally, the original language is followed, line by line, by the translation. Another approach is to place the texts side by side, matched for either sentences or short sections. If for some reason this is not done, at least accompany the translated text with a tape of the spoken words or give a reference to the tape's location.

## CORRECTING THE TRANSCRIPT

Once you or a transcriptionist has completed the first draft of the verbatim transcript, you must review it against the tape for accuracy. If you are transcribing your own tapes, you might do this section by section as you go. This saves time overall (even though it slows down the transcription somewhat) and tends to be more accurate. If you are using a transcriptionist, review the entire transcript carefully against the tape, listening for errors and making corrections as you go. Doing so can be time consuming, unless the transcriptionist is highly skilled, but it is essential. This is also a good point at which to insert further punctuation or any additional notes or contextual details you feel are necessary.

When you are reviewing the transcript against the tape, you will be listening with an ethnographer's ear. Ethnographic methods mean stripping away assumptions, cultural or personal, to observe—in this case, hear—precisely what occurs, whether or not it is entirely comprehensible. Interpretation and understanding come later. Listening in this way is exceptionally hard to do. The communicative urge means we "make sense" of speech all the time. We hear what we expect, whether or not it matches the sounds or the sense the speaker intended.

I want to illustrate this point with an excerpt from a transcription that was truly erroneous, to show how fallible the ear can be. Ellipses points in the excerpt indicate where considerable material was omitted because it was unproblematical; three-em underscores in square brackets indicate missing words. The following is the first draft of a transcription made by someone other than the interviewer:

> I bought—Monday morning is a big basket day, because people had ceremonies all weekend, because they work, see, this is James [_____] [ . . . ] Like I said, they have, ah, ceremonies over the weekend and then [_____], the medicine man [_____], I accept [_____] in [place name] we seem to have [_____], there seem to be [_____], a couple of them passed away.

The following is a second draft, corrected against the tape by the interviewer, with missing words filled in (I have underlined corrections):

> Monday morning is a big basket day, because people had ceremonies over the weekend, because they work, see, this <u>has changed</u> the whole dynamic of it. [ . . . ] Like I said, they have ceremonies over the weekend and then the medicine man—in [place name] we <u>just</u> seem to have [cannot hear 2–3 words] a couple of them <u>have</u> passed away.

The transcriptionist heard words that were not there ("I bought," "I accept," "ah," "there seem to be"), could not hear well what was there ("see, this has changed the whole dynamic of it" has been transcribed as "see, this is James"), and in many places was simply unable to hear the speech—hardly surprising since the interview had considerable background noise. As I was the interviewer, was familiar with the speaker's voice, and took notes, I was able to correct the transcript, although there was a phrase of two or three words that even I could not hear. In the final transcript, I inserted [?several, though] to help the sense of the narrative, but this was a considerable assumption on my part, and there are types of transcripts in which I would not do this. And that, too, is a point: we cannot help but make sense of what we hear, as the transcriptionist did when working on my tape. Ethnographic training teaches us to hear with, as it were, "open ears"—but even so we cannot help putting in meaning.

Computers make it easy to correct draft transcripts. Whether you listen to the tape while reading the screen or the printed text, make the corrections and print out the corrected version. This corrected version is the verbatim transcript, to be dated, saved as a document, and printed. In many cases this verbatim transcript is the final transcript. If that is the case, document it with relevant information (see chapter 4).

If the transcript is of an interview, you may have arranged for the person or persons you interviewed to review it, and in that event you may want to edit it first. In the next chapter, I discuss editing, its effects, and its role, especially in transcripts that will be reviewed. In chapter 5, I discuss the way in which people react to texts: no matter who it is, interviewees want to make their speech sound written.

# 4

# ON EDITING AND CONTEXT

Once the verbatim transcript is finished, including a thorough review and correction against the tape, the primary act of translation is done. Indeed, the verbatim transcript may be the final product you want. However, some transcripts require more work. You may need to add contextual information or notes on performance elements, and you might consider editing for readability and comprehension.

The very act of creating your verbatim transcript—distinguishing words from nonwords and deciding where to put commas and periods—is inherently a form of editing. A second sort of editing is that in which you alter a written transcript by cutting words, "correcting" grammar, making changes for readability, and sometimes even rewording, smoothing out the oral qualities of a written text. Since the transcript is already several steps from the original, should you edit at all?

As I have mentioned, a transcript is not a perfect copy of the spoken word—no more than is the tape recording. Both are reflections of the original reality, altered by the media through which they pass. One might ask, Why *not* edit, when the text is already removed from a vanishing reality? Perhaps you can preserve the oral flavor of the speech without including every nonword and false start. Oral historians work hard to produce readable texts that remain faithful to the original spoken content; why should ethnographers change this tested methodology?

Ethnographic methods depend on capturing events, including speech events, in the manner and environment in which they take place. For many ethnographers, transcripts provide quotations and illustrations for the explication of culture, usually in a fuller publication. At issue is how much you can edit a verbatim transcript and still be faithful to the spoken word. Any editing of such transcripts ought to be light and done with great care.

Your research goal and skills will underlie your decisions about whether to edit, what sort of editing to do, and how much of it is appropriate. Once again, the question is, What are your goals in producing a transcript?

One component of editing, however, is advisable for nearly all transcripts. That is the addition of notes about context. It is context that sets ethnographic methods apart—the importance of the social nexus, the spatial environment, and the interaction that takes place between speakers in a natural setting. But which context exactly?—there are many different kinds. You might need to describe, for example, the social and physical environment in which the recorded event took place, the cultural background of the speakers, and their styles of expression and expressiveness.

When we use ethnographic methods, we are trying to understand the varied ways people use words to communicate, to highlight some things and conceal others. We recognize the strategic, sometimes unconscious, uses of language that reflect social situations, dramatic performance, and religious ceremony. We note the ways people create puns, humor, insults, or flattery by subtle and not-so-subtle plays on words. A mixture of expression and context injects irony, respect, or insult into innocent-sounding words. And this is not even to approach the double meanings that so often make language rich.

Performance is what conveys much of this verbal art. Performance and its connections to verbal art and oral traditions are not truly the emphasis of this book. At the end of this chapter, however, after discussing editing and contextualizing, I include some tips for those who, in focusing on the spoken word, wish to know how to point up some aspects of performance.

## EDITING

Editing can be a creative activity, with all the positive and negative connotations that implies. The positive aspect of editing is that it makes clear what has been said. The negative aspect is that it changes another's words, indeed, polishing them so that they are no longer the words that were spoken. Editing a transcript should not be like editing a manuscript for publication.

Usually, editing consists of alterations, typically 1) word changes, often related to grammar; 2) deletions, of things such as false starts, nonwords, and repetitions; and 3) additions, of words or editorial comments that clarify or provide context.

There are basically only two reasons for editing transcripts. The first has to do with the way interviewees want their words to appear in a written text; the second has to do with how a text reads. In both cases, conveying the qualities of orality and "real" speech is a secondary goal, if it is a goal at all. Instead, the flow of the story is the chief concern. Pruning away nonwords and false starts, punctuating, and polishing grammar can enhance the core content of the interview, but the result will be distinctly different from most speech. As with everything else I suggest in this book, decide what you want your editing to accomplish and why. If your concern is speech, exactly as spoken, and your analysis relies on this precision, the only editing you should do is to use the conventions of writing well and consistently and to add whatever comments or contextual information you think necessary.

Many transcripts should *not* be edited. Transcripts that accompany videos as running captions, for example, are always verbatim. The members of a focus group, interested in group dynamics and the way they arrived at consensus or discord, might be best served by being given an unedited transcript to review. They will understand, or grasp quickly, the nature of a verbatim transcript. Other reviewers may already have a good sense of oral scripts or share the disciplinary focus of the research.

If you decide to edit, focus on your disciplinary needs. If your goal is to produce a text for ease of reading, narrative flow, and clear meaning rather than—or, better put, in addition to—capturing orality, you will be well aware that editing usually means making minor changes that clarify meaning, to the extent that it is clear to you. Pronouns can be especially confusing in transcripts. Attention to grammar and contextual comments is also useful: the speaker's revealing gestures and facial expressions, for example, can no longer be seen. There are times when edits or editorial comments help readers understand the transcript better.

In some cases, perhaps it would not be enough to tweak the spoken word—nothing short of radical rewriting would make the final text as comprehensible in writing as it would be in speech. Radical rewriting, though, is *not* a part of transcription (I discuss rewriting by an interviewee in chapter 5). When a transcript does not easily convey either clear meaning or a narrative, it should be left as it is. It may not be useful as a narrative text, but it may serve some other purpose, not least of which is to show that the research included each individual and what he or she said.

I want to distinguish between the editing done by researchers and the editing done by someone who has been interviewed and who later reviews the verbatim transcript. Interviewees will certainly regard the transcript as a textual, not an oral, document and will edit accordingly. They almost always want to be "corrected" for grammar. Though few of us speak like Shakespeare's characters or have Muhammad Ali's oral poetic style, we all want to speak fluently and "read well" on the page. It is the rare reader who can appreciate or even recognize the creativity of speech when it is transcribed exactly as it was spoken. Transcriptions lack all that made speech expressive and even understandable, so we tend to react as if the transcript were a weaker form of writing instead of a reflection of a complex form of communication.

Of all the people I have interviewed and asked to review the transcript, precisely two have ever resisted the urge to edit. If review is a necessary part of the process, then editing, too, may be necessary. In oral history, in interviews "for the record," and in some narratives, this may be appropriate. The editing should be a joint activity, especially when publication of transcripts is a goal of the research; the words are not exactly yours to change.

This is not an argument for editing, however. Indeed, the reactions of interviewees rather argue for the reverse: you may polish a transcript to whatever degree you like, and interviewees will still make changes. This is, of course, related to a sense of ownership, of possession, of their speech.

If you would like participants to review the transcript, but you also wish to capture something of the oral style of their speech, then tell them so. Explain what this entails and give them a sense of what they will see when they read the transcript. The goal of capturing actual spoken language in different situations is easy to explain, and if reviewers understand your research and goals, it may make a difference.

Overall, then, I recommend that when you edit, you do so lightly. For situations in which editing is either helpful or necessary, I discuss in the following sections the kinds of changes, omissions, and additions that are typical and what their benefits and drawbacks can be.

### The Parts of Oral Speech That Are Typically Edited

#### INCOMPLETE SENTENCES, PHRASES, REPETITIONS

In chapter 3, I discussed punctuation for partial sentences and used the following example, which included false starts, phrases, and repetitions:

> I started—started to run—run towards the group. I think I ran all the way. But I—when I got abreast of them, I stopped.

Could you appropriately take out some or all of the fragments? In a case such as this, you could do so with minimal changes:

> I started to run towards the group. I think I ran all the way. But when I got abreast of them, I stopped.

Is it the same speech? No. Is it acceptable? That is for you to decide.

Although editing is inappropriate for any transcript in which exact oral transcription is essential, the convention in narrative or other interviews is to edit out some or even all of the repetitions and some of the shorter or more incomprehensible unfinished phrases. Before doing so, ask yourself the following questions: Why do you want to remove the fragments? Is the repetition conscious, a use of style? Does the repetition, false start, or broken sentence indicate an important emotional context? By editing the fragments out, what will be lost—style, context, expression, or nothing much? For what kinds of research and analysis is it important to retain these fragments? For what kinds of research is it better to edit them out? By editing, will you gain clarity, meaning, or brevity?

If there are many partial sentences and phrases, you may need to edit them down to the comprehensible core, especially if you are transcribing a narrative. Use the speaker's own words rather than rebuilding or rewriting sentences. This is where your knowledge of both the recorded situation and the purpose of the transcript will drive the decision and where your analytical skills will come into play.

Edward Ives (1995:80) gave an example of editing in oral history, starting with the following verbatim transcript:

> Did I what uh, did I uh well, let me think uh yeah now sure, yeah sure I uh drove the uh uh the Kennebec River one no it was one spring yes.

Ives suggested transcribing the passage as follows:

> Well, let me think. Yeah, I drove the Kennebec River one spring.

He recommended explaining the transcription in a headnote, such as "Note [that the speech] was so full of hesitations, haltings, false starts and tag questions that occasionally I have had to exercise some judgment in deciding what to put in, what to leave out." He added that usually "such omissions can be taken for granted."

In an oral history interview, especially one reviewed by the interviewee and published or deposited in a public library or archive, this is acceptable editing and accepted practice. Yet I find it too radical for ethnographic methods. Nor do I believe that such omissions should be taken for granted. Here are a couple of ways I might handle the same sentence. First, I would punctuate it differently:

> Did I what—uh, did I—uh, well, let me think. Uh, yeah, now sure, yeah, sure—I, uh, drove the, uh, uh, the Kennebec River one—no, it was one spring, yes.

The change is minor, but it gives greater structure and coherence to the piece. If I were to edit further, I would omit the nonwords:

> Did I what—did I—well, let me think. Yeah, now sure, yeah, sure—I drove the—the Kennebec River one—no, it was one spring, yes.

My methodological position is that using ethnographic methods means altering speech minimally. Here, I believe added punctuation makes the verbatim text somewhat clearer and easier to read. The second edit is slight but gives polish. I would resist further editing, but if pushed, I might take out five words, as follows:

> Did I what—well, let me think. Yeah, now sure, yeah, sure—I drove the Kennebec River one—no, it was one spring, yes.

But is this editing essentially any different from Ives's version? I, too, have altered the text to make it something more articulate. Neither Ives's transcription nor mine reflects the original exactly. Although Ives's editing is more radical, the speaker's meaning is still intact and accessible. Does the reader of an oral history or any other sort of narrative or interview gain anything when a text replicates speech rather than meaning? This is a question for the researcher to address; my answer is that the spoken word has its own energy and direction, and my goal is to put it in writing. In my view, that is the difference between oral history and ethnographic methods.

Some speakers utter strings of false starts—multiple rephrasings of sentence beginnings—apparently rejecting all of them until finally a full sentence is produced that is clear and complete. This, too, is a form of editing—oral editing. If the point of your transcript is to produce a narrative for you to publish or quote, you may decide to edit out some false starts. If they appear throughout the interview, be consistent. You will be creating a succinct text that is not an oral record; the text is now becoming much more your creation, unless review is built into the process and the interviewee cooperates in creating the new text. In either case, your judgment will come into play, especially if you feel you need to retain some but not all phrases. You should, as usual, keep the verbatim version of the transcript as well as the edited one. You should also write a succinct note about your and your reviewer's editing at the beginning of the transcript or in its accompanying information.

In conversations or discussions among groups of people, speakers often talk in phrases rather than sentences, and the context and meaning of the phrases hinge on what the previous speaker said. In such cases, editing must not interrupt this flow; it would radically alter the exchange. Leave all the phrases as they are, whether or not their context is clear. If you need to publish or quote from the transcript, you can explicate the text accordingly for your readers. A discussion is a social interaction, not a set of individually segmented speech acts, and your text should capture that interaction.

Sometimes speakers' sentence constructions are very different from written structure. They may use nouns or verbs in unexpected ways, perhaps creating incomplete but fully intelligible sentences by omitting first-person pronouns:

> Don't know. Never tried it. Got in the habit of doing it my own way.

Some people leave sentences incomplete by allowing them to trail off at the end:

> And as I said, we didn't have any roads, there were no highways. But we did have about.... Let me see, Simpson's must have been...

I think the point to make is that transcripts are not written texts to edit for style. They are spoken words, and the work of turning them into writing ought not to include radical revisions for the mere sake of conforming to written formalities.

### FILLER WORDS

Speakers use all kinds of filler words, such as *well, right, you know, so*, and the current favorite, *like*. Although removing filler words does not alter the content of speech, it does alter the oral quality of the transcript. For example, removing "like" from the talk of those who use it regularly radically alters their speech. It may result in a form of the speech so truncated that it is hard to grasp. Yet if removing filler words does assist the narrative flow, it may not be so problematic.

The questions to ask are, Will this minor alteration of the style of speech alter the analysis? Is this alteration problematic or completely neutral? I recommend that you include fillers if style of speech is important in your work or if they are useful markers of gender, age, class, or region. If your goal is content, clarity, and brevity and if the filler words are numerous and obstruct meaning, then edit them out. Another solution is to include all filler words in the first page or paragraph and then edit them out in later passages, explaining this editing style in a parenthetical note. When you edit out fillers, you may find that you still have incomplete sentences, so ask yourself whether the improvement will be worth the effort.

In a narrative interview, length and readability are relevant issues. Eliminating filler words hardly changes length, but it may improve readability. Filler words can be mildly irritating—even in original speech. Your judgment and knowledge of goals are called for once again.

## NONVERBAL SOUNDS

Nonverbal sounds may also act as fillers, but they may instead convey meaning. Sometimes such sounds, variously spelled, indicate assent (uh-huh) or dissent (uhn-uhn). Sometimes speakers, especially interviewers, make such sounds to indicate interest, comprehension, or encouragement.

If the sound carries meaning, include it in your transcript. If the sound is a filler or indicates a pause without meaning, edit it out, unless your research focus requires its inclusion. Overlapping assents, especially on the part of an interviewer who may be showing interest or attention, may be cut, unless it is necessary to represent the full interaction in the transcript for analysis.

Laughter is another nonverbal sound you may want to edit in or out. If a speaker laughs rarely, annotate it in square brackets—[laughs]—when he or she does. Also annotate laughter if the transcript needs to indicate a speaker's style. If a speaker laughs frequently, however, merely as a filler, you could edit it out. In such a case, noting [laughter] each time becomes excessive. If the speaker's words are clearly humorous, you could use exclamation points (sparingly) to emphasize them. Again, be directed by your research goals.

## GRAMMAR

Spoken grammar differs from written grammar. It can be rich, articulate, and expressive, situated as it is in a wealth of contexts, facial expressions, gestures, and behaviors. In speech, word arrangements, uses of pronouns, subject–verb agreements, and so forth are structured differently than they are in writing; they need only make sense to the hearer, and formal grammar be damned.

Written grammar is about comprehension in a page of text. This is not the place to discuss meaning, intention, and whether these are communicated, whether hearers do understand exactly what the speaker intends. When it isn't clear, speakers ask questions. Or they follow up erroneous understandings; this is the basis of human drama, after all. Transcripts have to be very careful not to insert, or misinterpret, meaning. There are some exceptions to comprehension: in the language of very young children, people who are learning a second language, and people suffering from Alzheimer's disease, to name a few examples. Such people may well be the subjects of your study, in which case the exact replication of their forms of grammatical structure is important.

In general, though, interviewees, when they review their transcript, are concerned about formal grammar. In one oral history project I know of, a participant withdrew in disgust on reading the verbatim transcript, claiming she had been made to sound ignorant. The researcher perceived the language as imaginative and comprehensible; the interviewee saw only the difference with written language. However, after that, the researcher sent only edited transcripts to interviewees for review. I, too, have met with disappointment in people I interviewed who noticed only that I had not corrected their grammar when quoting from their transcripts.

If you edit, you need to decide whether you will always use standard forms of grammar or whether some exceptions are warranted. In the following example, the language, which does not follow written rules, is instantly clear, wonderfully direct:

> So everybody kind of sat down in their own spots, so I sat in this one guy's spot, you know, everybody has their own spot that they sit, so I went and sat in this one guy's, who always instigates some trouble, you know. [ . . . ] And from then on I had a lot of respect. Except for that one, that I didn't get back his seat to. Then finally, as years went by, that guy, [ ___ ] finally gave in and he said, "Oh man, you know, I would never believe how good of a worker you are."

I've left it exactly as it was spoken, with punctuation, and marks to show a cut section [ . . . ] and a name intentionally omitted [ ___ ]. I think it is entirely comprehensible, as the speaker—a woman discussing her first day as a miner—did when she reviewed it. It's also stylistically strong.

If you are editing and find that the spoken grammar is getting in the way of understanding the text, the solution may sometimes be simple: changing a verb to agree with a subject, adding a pronoun, converting an adverb into an adjective, or supplying punctuation. If your methods require precision, you could place such edits in square brackets to show that they are your words, not the speaker's. Here's an example of a short section in which editing might help the reader:

> And then this girl, she helped me to tie that guy up. And then we took in the hay barn. He was in there, and then there was another guy came along. I guess he untied that one, and then he take off with the rope on his back.

In context of the entire speech, this is reasonably clear, but some editing helped:

> And then this girl, she helped me to tie that guy up. And then we took [him] into the hay barn. He was [tied up] in there and then there was another guy came along. I guess he untied that one [the first man], [who] took off with the rope on his back.

Sometimes the solution is far more complex. You may not know what the speaker meant precisely enough to make good changes. You may feel that only radical changes will solve the problem, and so you are faced with opposite choices: total rewriting or simply making minor changes in sentences that are still ungrammatical.

The best solution is never clear. If you radically rewrite, you will lose some integrity in the speech as well as running the risk that you have misunderstood the speaker's meaning or intent. If you do not rewrite, the speech may convey little meaning to the reader. If you cannot be sure, leave it as it is. You have maintained an important methodology, keeping the words verbatim and not attempting an interpretation. If you have a sense of what the speaker was trying to say, you might add an editorial note in brackets giving your reading of it, but be sure to note that this is your interpretation, as in this example:

> And then I guess some of them, their grandkids and their kids scared them, if they don't make direct deposit, they won't get their check no more. [Social Security checks, I think she means. She was discussing the problem of bank accounts, deposits, and getting cash on the Navajo Reservation.]

## AMBIGUOUS PRONOUNS

One element of spoken grammar that particularly affects meaning and is often unclear is the use of ambiguous pronouns. We often use pronouns loosely when speaking, which can create confusion in a written transcript:

> The second one was Cora's work. [ . . . ] She had done Rorschach tests there, and that was the subject matter of that.

If you were present at the recorded event, you may have made notes, or you may know from context or expression who or what is being referred to. In transcribing, I added this information in square brackets: ". . . and that was the subject matter of that [her dissertation]."

Some of the pronouns that appear in speech are simply misspoken—*she* for *he*, and vice versa, is common. More complicated is the appearance of identical pronouns referring to either of two people:

> My father and my brother were both in the army. He went in in '48.

This might be clear to the interviewer, who knows from the age of the speaker that she is talking about her father, but the transcript should make it clear to readers in a parenthetical note: "He [father] went in in '48." The speaker continues:

> We grew up in a military household, you might say. He served in the reserves, and then he went off to war. We didn't expect that.

As it turns out, both pronouns in the second sentence refer to the speaker's brother, but we learn this only through context as the interview continues. The interviewer does not ask for clarification. How is the reader to know? Such confusion of pronouns is common. When you learn whom the speaker is referring to, add the reference in brackets: [speaker's father] or [speaker's brother]. When it is unclear and when the interviewer has not tried to clarify the matter, either at the time or later, you have no choice but to leave the pronouns as they are.

In analyses that focus on meaning, interpretation, misinterpretation, or use of pronouns, in which attention is paid to the very manner in which people speak and do or do not make themselves clear, always transcribe the exact words people said. In short, for all analyses that focus on verbal communication and the use of words, verbatim is the only possible form of transcription. In such cases it may be unnecessary to make any additions or clarifications.

### Cuts and Deletions: What to Omit, When, and How

Depending on the purpose of a transcript, a researcher may decide to delete from the verbatim version material that falls outside his or her research focus. For example, someone who is studying child language and creating a transcript from which to analyze such speech might find that a verbatim record of instructions given to the child's mother, or discussions with her, while relevant to the research, are unnecessary in the transcript. The instructions might be condensed into a brief summary presented at the beginning of the transcript, and the mother's comments, if useful, might be mentioned in a note. As long as the full instructions are included as part of the overall research notes and records, there is no need to transcribe this section verbatim. Here is an example, a fragment of my own speech that was recorded when I turned on the tape recorder and that I would cut from the final transcript:

> Yes, I am very well aware of this. Don't want to get involved in it but, needless to say some of this is going to be part of the story. I may choose not to tell it, but I am going to hear it.

The interviewee had been chatting, irrelevantly before we began the tape, somewhat irrelevantly, about other people, but in fact I had not begun the interview. Many similar situations will arise in which recorded material is tangential to the goals or methods of the research; as always, let your research purposes guide your decisions to omit or include it.

Another category of material that may be deleted during editing is conversation that is irrelevant to the research focus. Recorded events are not always neatly bracketed into "talk for research" and "other talk." Interviews often contain considerable conversation not directly related to the interview. Often, interviewers turn the tape recorder off for such essentially irrelevant friendly chatter, but if you identify such conversation in your verbatim transcript, you may want to edit it out for the final transcript. Other kinds of speech sessions that must be recorded in full may also contain irrelevant material. How should you determine what constitutes chat and banter and what is essential to discussion? If a focus group of four people is taped, for example, for the purposes of recording a decision-making process, and if two or more of the participants spend a few minutes discussing a football game they have watched, can you cut this section? If the point of the transcript is to capture the process of decision making, then mentioning this portion of chat in a note or cutting it altogether makes sense. If the research is aimed at showing the full range of exchange and the building of partnerships, then presenting the entire process and the way it evolved, detoured, or went off track may be relevant. In any case, if you make a cut, always note that you have done so.

If you ask a transcriptionist to make cuts or omit material, your instructions must be very precise. For instance, if you want all remarks made by a researcher to be cut, request that the cuts be noted in square brackets. You may want simply to note cuts: [ . . . ], or you may ask for a phrase that mentions the topic [researcher talks about weather], [ Jones asks question about ___ ], or something similar. You might request that the tape counter be given at the point of the cut and again at the end. If you want just those remarks that are "chatter"—that is, off the questions of the research—to be cut, you will need to be sure the transcriptionist has a good grasp of what constitutes on- and off-message remarks by both researchers and participants. In some cases it is easier and does not take much longer to get a full verbatim transcript and then cut it yourself.

Publication style guides generally recommend showing the omission of words in a text by inserting three dots, or ellipsis points. I used them, in brackets, for that purpose in an earlier example: "The second one was Cora's work. [ . . . ] She had done Rorschach tests there." If you are cutting only a nonword such as *um* or a filler word such as *like*, you can dispense with this notation.

### Additions

On some occasions you will want to add an editorial comment such as [the following has been edited for easier reading]. Square brackets are the universal convention for indicating material that has been added by someone other than the original speaker—or writer, in the case of text.

If a sentence when it is written down is unclear but you or the transcriber knows what was meant or intended, you could insert either a word or a revised phrasing for clarification in square brackets, as some of the previous examples illustrate. If neither you nor the transcriber (or interviewer, if this was a third person) clearly understands what was meant and you want the reader to know this, it may be helpful to add something like [not clear to transcriber] or [meaning unclear here]. You can leave the sentence as it is, in all its original obscurity, but without a note of explanation, readers (or even you some years later) may be uncertain about what is going on. Is text missing? Is the reader missing something? In annotating unclear passages, however, do not use terms such as [garbled] or [incomprehensible]. What seems garbled or incomprehensible to the hearer will undoubtedly not have been so to the speaker. Be careful with comments; if noting [speaker mumbles], for example, be sure that the speaker *did* mumble and it is not just your inability to hear.

If a speaker mutters—that is, speaks to himself in a low voice so that you cannot hear—this is a different situation. It becomes a matter of intention on the speaker's part and interpretation on yours. It's also an interesting issue: Can you be certain? If the speaker didn't intend you to hear, should you transcribe the material, especially if you *didn't* hear it fully? Or is the speaker expressing hostility or some other emotion? The intersection of meaning, intention, and interpretation is full of fuzzy boundaries. Exercise caution and listen carefully. If the tape goes something like this,

> Speaker: [unclear words]
> Researcher: I'm sorry, I didn't hear.
> Speaker: Nothing.

there may well be something going on. But is it right to insert [mumbles]? Let your skills and goals be your guide.

## CONTEXT

A vital component in editing a transcript is to contextualize it—to annotate it with background information that gives you, during later analysis, or other readers a better sense of the larger scene. It is context that sets ethnographic methods apart. Ethnographers want to see the surrounding world, the social nexus, the spatial environment, and the interactions of speakers in a natural setting. Transcripts—mere texts—are not going to reflect full context no matter how much we add and annotate. Just as a photograph fails to capture the entire picture, we inevitably lose the depth of oral exchanges when we transfer them to writing. Yet transcripts should convey *some* contextual richness; we know that writing has its own powerful creativity.

The question is, Which contexts can one try to capture in a transcript? I want to discuss two kinds of contexts: that of the recording that is being transcribed (who, what, when, and where) and that which is embedded within the recording. This does not exhaust the topic of context, particularly in linguistic analysis, where context can be different things in different research (see Duranti and Goodwin 1992). For such analyses, a specialized transcription notation is needed, which exceeds the scope of this book.

### Introductory Contextual Information

Every transcript should have introductory information that gives specifics about the event, its participants, its location, and the research. Even if the only user is yourself, such an introduction is an aid to memory, a condensation of your notes and observations, for future years when you may not remember as much as you think you will. If you are going to the trouble of creating a transcript, you may well want to return to it or let others use it later on.

In this introduction, which might be a cover page, record the details of who, where, when, what, and why. I have seen transcripts in archives that fail to provide such context. They might give the goal of the project but only the name of the interviewee, without any biographical details (which might become clear in the interview but should be given up front), not even the person's gender—not all first names clearly indicate this. Often, the interviewer is not mentioned at all. I believe a few details should be given about the researcher—yourself or any other interviewer who is actively engaged in the activity being recorded, even if it is just the person's title, affiliation, or role. This is context, and it is critical.

Most important, in recording any activity that you will transcribe later, plan to take notes or have someone else do so, naming each speaker and writing down the first few words he or she says. This is crucial for transcribing. It is not always possible to recognize people's voices on tape, even if you know them and were there. If you have someone else do the transcribing, such notes are essential (see chapter 2).

The basic contextual details you should provide are the following:

- The date, time, place, and event being recorded.
- The names and roles of everyone involved in the transcript, including the interviewer and other researchers who speak. You might also give a thumbnail biography for each person. In the case of an interview, it is especially important to provide biographical information about the interviewee: the person's approximate age or information that places him or her in an age-group (elementary school student, retired teacher, longtime engineer). Summarize information given in the recording, such as culture group, or work-related, religious, or political affiliations.
- In the case of a discussion or other event with several people, a summary of who the participants were.
- A brief explanation of the reason the activity was carried out, recorded, and transcribed. If it was part of a project, include the project title and the name of the principal investigator, any institutional affiliation, and the beginning and end dates of the project.

You may also want to name the transcriber if it was someone other than yourself. Since you are ultimately responsible for reviewing and correcting the transcript, this is less critical, unless you did not actually compare the transcript with the tape. You may want to note whether the transcript is a "verbatim, unedited," "slightly edited," or "fully edited" version.

*Context within the Recorded Event*

During the course of recording, many things can go on. Even an interview has interruptions: other people enter the room, a telephone rings, a train thunders past. In any exchange, there may also be moments when furniture, features of the landscape or streetscape, objects, or photographs, not to mention the other people involved in the activity, become "props"—that is, they are referred to or are indicated by gestures or in some other way. A transcriber can handle such things by adding comments about them in square brackets: [phone rings], [father enters room; greets child and leaves], or [points to a photograph of her mother].

Features in the landscape or streetscape often play a role in the recorded event. The introduction to the transcript should give event's locale. If the event was *about* these external features—an interview about the history of a building, for example—state as precisely as possible the relevant geographic locations and names of features (hills, rivers, streets, buildings) and provide cross references to maps, prints, or videos that exist separately. If, however, these features play into the speech in more general, metaphorical, or symbolic ways, you will probably note the contextual details as [nods at street crossing], [extends arms to the landscape], or other, similar comments.

When people are recorded talking about landscapes, sites, or streetscapes, they are often walking through or looking at the scene being discussed. If the main intention of the recording is to capture geographic or site-specific information and history, there are usually accompanying videos and photographs. Today's technology can incorporate digitized still images into transcripts. Geographic Information Systems (GIS) technology will be useful here. When such contextual information cannot be provided digitally, describe—briefly but precisely and in as much detail as the situation merits—the landscape and/or the spot where the recording took place and note compass directions for specific features.

When a speaker refers to a specific feature of the landscape or to a material prop, identify the item in square brackets:

> As I sit here, I look at the dancers up there on the mural [on the wall is a mural showing a green corn dance, painted in 1931 by Oqwapi (Abel Sanchez) of San Ildefonso] and I think about how we do things. (Powers 2005:133)

The sorts of props that might appear in a recorded event are legion. People often use photographs as aids to memory, and objects are often topics of discussion—say, pieces of jewelry, books, or car parts. Even if you have prepared to take notes about what they are or to take photographs of them, it is still extremely easy to lose track of which particular item or photograph is being discussed. Videotaping resolves many of the problems since it can record objects and speech simultaneously. But if the transcript is not going be read together with the video, then incorporate into the transcript, if possible, a photograph (a digital image or photocopy) of the item or photograph under discussion.

If photographs are used in interviews, it's helpful if they are numbered beforehand and the number is mentioned in the taped discussion. Yet good intentions often fade as people's interest in the contents of the images increases. It is helpful to prepare spare photocopies of the images ahead of time and to keep notes on them during the discussion, either numbering them in the order in which they are discussed or noting the time or the tape counter on each one. If this cannot be done, at least take good notes on what each image is as it is discussed. Later, ask whether you may borrow the photographs to make photocopies of them.

If you do obtain photocopies or digital images of other people's photographs, remember that you will not have copyright to them. Should you need to publish them, you will need to obtain specific permission to do so; unless you have specified this, it will not be part of the interview permission form.

## PERFORMANCE AND POETRY

A special category of transcription—that of performances—demands much greater editing and contextualizing than most others. Performances might be events such as a storytelling (indoors, outside, on a stage, and so on), a griot's recitation, a drama or a pageant with actors (also in many environments), a poetry reading, an exchange of humorous or bawdy stories, and so on. Much of performance is difficult, if not impossible, to capture in writing in its entirely. This may seem to be the case for *all* speech, and indeed in some theoretical approaches, all cultural action and spoken communication is framed as "performance" (see, for example, Goffman 1983). Different researchers espouse different conceptions of performance; for a range of them, I recommend reading works by Richard Bauman (1986), Elizabeth Fine (1984), and Ruth Finnegan (1992).

In one approach, "acts of communication are somehow marked out as performance by a heightened and framed quality" (Finnegan 1992:91), whether these acts are formal (performed, say, in a theater or a village square), informal (stories or anecdotes told to friends), or something in between. Examining performance from this perspective would undoubtedly require a videotape. If a transcript is a necessary addendum to the video, ask yourself what purposes it will serve and what details should be included.

A good way to think of representing performance in text may be as a script, much like a script for a play or film, with comments inserted about people's movements, gestures, and facial expressions and about any other relevant actions or contexts. There is an important difference, of course: theater scripts are meant to be interpreted differently by different directors, whereas transcripts are meant to be representations, as faithful to a particular original event as possible, combining description and verbatim text.

The translation of oral style—all the elements of expression, phrasing, and tone—in a performance transcript is perhaps even more challenging than it is in other kinds of transcripts. Performance includes so much that is vital yet cannot easily be translated into writing: irony, atmosphere, the interplay of sound and words, dramatic or poetic phrasing, tone of voice to display emotion, the sound effects of repetitions, the personalities of the performers, the switch of a performer into different roles or "voices"—the list continues (Finnegan 1992:91–94).

It is always helpful to remember that a transcript is always a watered-down notation that contributes what it can to future analysis or the preservation of some details. Decide which details, then, are essential, which are useful, and which can—however reluctantly—be left out for your particular purposes. Remember that the tape or video is there also. And, in all transcriptions of performances, be sure to follow ethical guidelines and get appropriate permissions; the material is other people's intellectual property.

Here are some points to consider as you make decisions about whether and how to transcribe performances:

- Videotapes (as currently being made—see chapter 5) will not last long, and paper documents will. Is preservation (of words, of the whole performance) the goal, or is it current analysis?
- If preservation is the goal, is a script the best model for the transcript?
- If discussion or analysis is the goal, is the text for words only? If so, how much, if any, of the most expressive, dramatic, and contextual information may be omitted?
- Is the performance being recorded for replay to other audiences? If so, the transcript may not need to be a script that includes expressive and other elements.

*Annotating Performance Transcripts*

Mode of expression is an important part of any performance, from storytelling to a ceremony with hundreds of participants. Pitch, loudness, and vocal tone might be used to indicate, for example, voices other than that of the protagonist or narrator. These will be captured by audio- and videotape, but your observations, notes, and memory will be helpful in transcribing them. If you need to annotate the words of a performance according to these elements, the contextual additions may be extensive: [her voice rising], [loudly], [sarcastically], and so forth. You might set such contextual information apart in the way text is laid out or by using different typefaces. You might even create a separate document for contextual information, with a system to key the description to the transcribed text.

If the performance has an audience, describe it, including its approximate size, and include its reaction to the performance and its voiced or physical interactions with the performers. You can give brief but specific descriptions by using the audience as a speaker—"Audience: Aaaah"—or through the voice of a (usually nameless) person: "Man in the audience cries: Stop her!" Or you might just insert bracketed comments such as [boos], [laughter], [rhythmic clapping on left side of audience], [murmur runs through audience], or [silence]—the last, for example, after a pause or joke or at the end of a piece. The range of descriptive notes can be as extensive as the event.

Note also the cultural context of the voiced audience interaction: not all hisses may be negative, for example, and some audiences join in to provide sounds for the performer. Some vocalizations may have no standardized spellings; others may be difficult to hear or grasp. Still others might be traditional responses, either in an archaic language or in onomatopoeia with (or without) a standardized spelling.

If you want to include details about movement, entrances and exits, or gestures, you may want to give these in somewhat the same way as a script for a play or film provides them. In a transcript such annotations, like all other contextual comments, should be placed in square brackets. This is not done in a script, but in a transcript these are not instructions from a playwright but descriptions by an observer. In addition to describing the setting and the characters involved, their movements, entrances, and exits, note basic layout and perhaps orientation (north, south, facing or backed by light, and so on). A sketch may be useful as well. How much you describe depends on your project goals and the way in which you involve participants, who may have other elements of description to suggest.

Again, your intended use or purpose of a textual transcript will determine what you want to include. As you make decisions, continually return to the goals of your research, recording, and transcription and the reasons you decided a transcription, rather than or in addition to the original recording, was needed.

*Poetry*

The reading or recitation of poetry is a distinctive form of speech, though it may occur in conjunction with music or as part of a dramatic performance. We think of it as expressive, yet poetry reading often employs traditional tones of voice that do not always "express" the poem's content. For example, a recording by Ezra Pound of his own poetry has, to my ears, the ring of a New England preacher or an old-style lecturer. Though this is not the current mode, a distinctive "tone" for poetry readings in English continues to exist—a relatively uninflected, even unemotional tone in which cadences are patterned and recognizable. Each culture has its own stylistic mode for poetry performance, specific to the type of poetry being performed. There are few good ways to get such traditional-style presentations across other than to describe them and to remember that the tape provides it best.

In chapter 3, I discussed volume and emphasis; the two can be indicated in combination by using capital letters and repeating vowels: "NooooOOOO." Dennis Tedlock's book *Finding the Center: Narrative Poetry of the Zuni Indians* (1972) illustrates his method for transcribing poetry. He explains it usefully in the introduction (pp. xv–xxxii), and the subsequent transcripts illustrate his method. Other sources for looking at the transcription of poetry or poetic stories include Ellen B. Basso's *Kalapo Myth and Ritual Performance* (1985). Basso carefully represents stress, onomatopoeic sounds, and reported speech (though she does not include volume, perhaps because there was little variation in her informants' speech).

It is common, in prose as well as poetry, to indent lines to reflect the speaker's phrasing and pauses. Electing to use this convention will relate to the speaker's style, but it clearly involves interpretation and should be done with caution. Dennis Tedlock discusses phrasing by indenting lines in *The Spoken Word and the Work of Interpretation* (1983:56–61).

These, then, are the additional, often challenging, always creative aspects of completing a transcript. Though they are not always necessary—I, for example, edit very little, and do not include expressive context (nor have I transcribed performances)—they will be important in some circumstances, for certain types of work. Providing context and documenting the transcript—which I do, especially for those transcripts that go to an archives—is almost always necessary. Given the fact that transcribing is hard work, these professional additions give transcripts some methodological strength and add to their useful longevity.

*5*

# THE SOCIAL RELATIONS
# OF TRANSCRIPTS

Like everything else in ethnography, transcripts come with social relation-ships—relationships, that is, among all the people involved in making them, whether speakers, researchers, transcribers, or users. The social aspects of making a transcript include each person's responsibilities, their face-to-face interactions and reactions, the working rapport that may or may not follow from these interactions, and the differing goals of all concerned.

Built into the relationships between researchers and participants are eth-ical and often political concerns that underlie who should have a say in the production and control of words. Such concerns come into play most force-fully in the case of interviews and performances, where protocols may require review of a transcript by participants and the need to consider intellectual property issues. Contracts may be required; permission forms certainly will be; and verbal agreements will be made about who does what. The formal relationships between the interviewer or researcher, those being recorded or interviewed, the recorder, and the transcriptionist (if the last two are not also the interviewer or researcher) include the roles, responsibilities, and activities each participant has discussed and agreed to. The informal relationships are those we might call the chemistry and interactions of people sharing, how-ever briefly, a common place, time, and activity. These relationships always have an influence on the outcome of the work. However cut-and-dried and predictable the formal responsibilities may be, unpredictability is the nature of human beings and contributes to the delights and surprises of working together. Knowing some of the factors in advance, however, can help reduce unpleasant surprises for everyone.

In this chapter, I go over the relationships between the interviewer or re-searcher and the other people involved in creating a transcript—transcribers, interviewees, and users of the written text. What should they expect from each other, and how might they best work together? How can the finished transcript best be preserved and made accessible to future users? Each project will differ and will include many situations and specifics not covered here. I offer only the basic ingredients.

## RESEARCHER AND TRANSCRIPTIONIST

Skilled transcriptionists are hard to find and thus expensive, and they should be. Many researchers use students or anyone else who is available and more or less efficient with a keyboard. Whoever does the transcribing, you, the researcher, will guide the transcript and ensure that it is methodologically sound and prepared according to your wishes and explicit decisions. A few transcriptionists—individuals rather than employees of transcription services—will evaluate a tape by listening to a portion and will advise the client about whether it is especially challenging in sound quality or other factors and therefore will be more costly to transcribe. I strongly recommend that every researcher transcribe at least a small portion of one tape in a project in order to get a full sense of the special needs of the work, its level of difficulty, and what sorts of decisions you need to make.

*Using Professional Transcriptionists*

### FOR THE RESEARCHER

The researcher or interviewer who hires a professional transcriptionist is responsible for guiding the transcription. Even if your transcriptionist has his own style guides and provides you with a guide on which to list your preferences, and even if the issues he raises are similar or identical to those raised in this book, you must outline your own points, methods, and specific instructions. You need to select these details according to a set of methods that relate to the work you are doing, and you must do everything you can to make the professional's work efficient.

Most professional transcriptionists have considerable experience with tapes prepared by a broad variety of people: oral historians, sociologists, educational researchers, lawyers, anthropologists, and representatives of many other disciplines. When contracting with someone new, ask about her clients' professions and, if necessary, ask whether you may contact a reference in your discipline or field of interest. Professional transcriptionists tend to prefer to transcribe interviews rather than recordings of discussion or focus groups because different voices and overlapping speech are difficult to handle if one was not present. They are also time consuming and thus expensive since most professionals charge by the page.

Transcriptionists should receive guidelines from those who give them work. It appears, however, that they are rarely asked about their methods, and as a result some have drawn up lists of questions for their clients to respond to—questions that relate to the client's preferences for formatting, style, spelling, and other elements. Most will use one of the professional style guides, such as the *Chicago Manual of Style,* but they may ask about your preference in such guides. Give transcriptionists all the information they need to produce a text in the format you need, using the options you have chosen for verbatim production and, if you have decided on it, any as-you-go editing. Also provide information that will assist their understanding, including how to spell personal names and place-names, and any special references they may need to consult. Tell them how you want to receive the transcripts—on a floppy disk, on a CD, in hard copy, or in some combination thereof. You will need to make a set of good copy tapes since using a tape in transcription creates wear and tear, and the original must be kept for reference. If a videotape is being used for transcription, the challenges are greater, as I discuss later.

Planning is important when a discussion or other group activity is recorded and will be transcribed (see chapter 2). Transcriptionists will need considerable assistance; it is even better if transcriptionists can be identified before the event and can attend it. Unless you have provided good notes or the discussion is videotaped, they are unlikely to be able to identify each speaker. Overlapping speakers are particularly difficult to hear and transcribe. Notes are essential.

Form 1 in appendix A is designed for use in outlining methods and preferences to give to a transcriptionist; form 2 covers formatting information. The transcriptionist may have other questions and needs; make sure these fit the methods you want and add them to the outline. If you have not used the transcriptionist before, you might ask to see a page or two before the whole text is completed.

FOR THE PROFESSIONAL TRANSCRIPTIONIST

You may have your own list or form that you give clients. However, if the client is a social scientist or someone else using ethnographic methods and does not specify transcription methods, you might give him form 1 in appendix A and ask him to fill it out. It is specifically designed to walk the researcher through notations and decisions he or she should think about before giving you a tape to transcribe. The form is intended to make the client recognize the challenges you, the transcriptionist, face and to remind her of the disciplinary elements she should be familiar with and should specify in a transcript.

*Using Student or Other Nonprofessional Transcriptionists*

FOR THE RESEARCHER

Transcribing is an excellent opportunity for students. It exposes them to all the richness of the spoken word and to the issues and ideas related to language, both oral and written. It gives them experience in learning to listen to the way speech is produced. It is also an excellent opportunity for you to teach, train, and ensure that the student gets as much from the work of transcribing as he or she would from a methods course. I can think of no better way to teach issues of language and some of the methods used in studying it than this hands-on, guided activity.

Although hiring students or other nonprofessionals may save you money and some time, the results will not necessarily be exactly what you need. Your efforts, however, can help the student transcriptionist to produce what you want, especially when more than one transcript is required and the same person is working on all of them. If you are using several transcriptionists, then your planning and communication can help them to produce relatively similar products.

Be sure your instructions to the student transcriptionist are clear, specific, and written down. Illustrate your requirements with examples. When requesting a dash, for instance, be explicit about the kind of dash you want. In one case where I requested a dash, it was rendered as ___ rather than —, a minor but irritatingly time-consuming error to correct.

Asking student transcriptionists to call if they have queries is helpful but not always productive. They may be reluctant to call you, and you are busy. They may not have queries. Or they may try to be helpful. I asked one student to leave a blank for Navajo words but not to try to transcribe them because he was unfamiliar with the language. He did so anyway, with results that were, alas, not useful. Discussing methods and their rationale, value, and efficiency will aid in laying useful groundwork in methodology and prevent everyone's frustration. It helps to have a transcriptionist who is communicative and to be able to use the same transcriptionist for a set of transcripts—but students are busy, too.

You will always need to review tapes against transcripts, no matter who does the work, but you will probably spend more time checking and correcting student transcripts than those made by professionals. If you have not worked with the student on transcribing before, ask to review the first few pages before he or she continues. Although correcting isn't difficult, especially with an electronic document (perhaps in conjunction with a printed version), you will save time and trouble if you have been very specific about your requirements and methods and if you review a segment of the transcript at the beginning. Supply the student with floppy disks or CDs to ensure that these are not old or corrupted and with paper if you require a printed version.

Besides saving money and time, a benefit to using student transcriptionists is that during your careful, more time-consuming review of the first draft, you may also be able to index the transcript for your work. You may have decided to edit to some degree, and this, too, could be done as you review if it consists of things such as removing nonwords or repetitions and making some cuts. However, always keep the original draft of the verbatim transcript. If the student is accurate, keep the original document; if there are many errors or gaps of unheard words, correct the transcript first and keep your corrected version.

Sometimes family members or friends (without experience, that is) offer or are asked to transcribe tapes. Skills are there to be learned, and willingness and interest are essential basics, as is knowing how to use a computer. As always, make sure your instructions are clear, specific, and written down. As before, go over the first few pages of transcript as soon as they are completed. Make sure to give a realistic deadline. Discuss your work, your expectations, and the spoken word as it relates to transcription. Unless the volunteer shows real enthusiasm for the work of transcribing and a determination to do it right—and perhaps even when these are present—this may not be an ideal situation.

FOR THE STUDENT TRANSCRIPTIONIST

Transcribing can be an excellent way to learn about language and methods. As I note previously, it exposes you to the richness of the actual spoken word as well as to the concepts and issues in language, oral and written. It is hard work, but it is definitely interesting for those who want to learn about the many styles of speech, its production and variation, and human interaction and communication. It will teach you how to listen well. The work will broaden your experience, especially if the recording is in your particular discipline or area of interest. It also offers insights into interviewing; you will have an invaluable opportunity to compare and critique styles and to learn from what you hear.

You will need guidelines, and until you get them, do not start transcribing. Appendix A offers a form that the researcher should fill out for you. There is more to transcribing than meets the eye; it may not be rocket science, but neither are its methods transparently obvious. Assume nothing and read this book.

Last, make sure you learn something through transcribing. If, when you have completed a transcript, you understand more about ethnographic and transcription methods; about the wealth of expression in human speech; about its ability to be communicative, puzzling, poetic, and varied; as well as something about the difference between written and spoken speech, between orality and textuality, then your work will have been worthwhile for your own development. If you are getting nothing from it, don't continue.

*What the Transcriptionist Should Get from the Researcher*

1. A set of copy tapes
2. Instructions for all the points discussed in chapter 3 (see appendix A, form 1)
3. All formatting instructions (including word-processing program and document names) in writing (see appendix A, form 2)
4. If necessary, the name of the publication style guide to be referred to
5. Specifications for the form or forms in which the transcript is to be produced: on a CD, on a floppy disk, in hard copy, and so forth (see appendix A, form 2)
6. Brief information (verbal or written) about the project or the research and about the goals of the transcript
7. A written list of the names of people (and, if necessary, places) mentioned on or participating in the recording
8. Information about any languages or technical terms used in the tape and the reference for a dictionary or other source for these terms. (If the source is a hard-to-find item, it should be provided.) Languages with which the transcriptionist may be unfamiliar should be mentioned and the method for handling them discussed.

## RESEARCHER AND PARTICIPANTS

The major engagement of the participants in a recorded speech event may lie in the event itself. In some cases, however, creating a transcript will continue their involvement. Many types of research focus on something other than individuals or produce transcripts intended for use only in conjunction with the activities recorded, not for publication. In these cases, having participants review the transcript is unnecessary. At other times, obtaining such a review will be part of your methods and procedures.

Review is especially necessary when all or part of the transcript is to be published. Some are ethnographic biographies (see Gelya Frank's *Venus on Wheels* [2000]), works that include biographical interviews to give depth and detail to history (Don Freedman and Jacqueline Rhoads's *Nurses in Vietnam* [1987], and all the works of Studs Terkel), and publications of recorded discussions (R. T. Grele's *Envelopes of Sound* [1985]). The benefit of having participants review transcripts is that errors of fact, hearing, or interpretation can be caught by those involved. Further, researchers and participants can discuss matters that might be too sensitive, private, or culturally unacceptable to be published.

The most important point to make about participants' relationships to transcripts is that in some cases the document will become, in today's self-aware and property-conscious world, "intellectual property." We share our spoken words easily, but once they are set down in writing, we may want to claim them as our own or guard them from misuse. When publication is involved (as well as when it is not), issues of intellectual property rights arise, along with issues of giving proper credit or assuring anonymity. These matters are best addressed not at the point of transcription review but before the recording begins (see chapter 2).

*Reviewing: The Sight of Speech*

Many people are unfamiliar with the sight of speech, and reading a verbatim transcript may come as a surprise, if not a shock. Some, whether or not they are familiar with verbatim transcripts, will take every opportunity to "correct" their spoken words, revising exactly as they would any other text—whether the researcher welcomes the revisions or not. Academics, myself included, edit the most extensively. Perhaps this is partly because we want to correct impressions or details, but we also seem simply unable to leave written texts untouched. Everyone, though, makes changes. I often find that people want to remove the "oral" aspects of a transcript altogether.

Sometimes it's unclear exactly what the rationale for the changes is. In one long interview I carried out that had been very satisfying to both parties, the transcript was returned with virtually every word changed. I have heard of other interviewers whose transcripts had not merely words but entire contents altered, producing an entirely different narrative—in one case, the reverse of the first interview. I'll return later to ways in which you might handle such situations.

Conducting a participant review of a transcript is always time consuming. You and the reviewer will inevitably have different timetables. Participants might ignore the task for more pressing concerns or, conversely, might carry it out so enthusiastically that they devote endless time to it. You will probably want to specify a deadline, but if you absolutely need the review, you may have to extend the deadline many times. If the review is both ethical and necessary, as in the case of a narrative interview that is to be deposited in an archive or used extensively in a book or exhibit, then maintaining good relationships with the participant may necessitate several visits to his or her home. Participants may find that they enjoy these meetings so much that they wish to prolong them, or they may find them so tedious that they try to avoid them—and all points on that continuum.

## FULL VERBATIM TRANSCRIPTS

Even when, following all my prescriptions for light editing, you have produced a transcript that you feel captures the flavor and essence of the interviewee's speech and intent, you may well find that he or she is not nearly as pleased with it as you are. Here lies a very real divergence of goals and desires as well as the basic difference between the oral and the written. Your goal may be to capture speakers' words, styles, and meanings; theirs may be to make particular statements or narratives and to ensure that they read well on paper. Working with reviews of a transcript offers as full an insight into the interface between the oral and the written as you will ever get.

Indeed, what is spoken has a unique quality, half ephemeral, half concrete, both personal and public, wholly serious but a record for fewer witnesses than a document is. Once committed to paper, our words take on a different aspect; losing expression, they seem to escape from the meaning we thought we'd given them. We no longer own them in quite the same way, yet our name is attached to them. Depending on the context, we may feel more possessive of or more cautious about texts than about speech. This is the nature of the interface between the oral and the written, and it is an interface with a long history. Present someone with a transcript of what he or she said, and you will see the issues surrounding this interface very clearly.

When a verbatim transcript is to be reviewed, you need first to gauge the kind of editing to do in order to present the transcript to the speaker. In one project in which verbatim transcripts were sent to all interviewees, one participant was quite upset by the sight of his speech. When people compare the transcripts of their speech to a good book or, say, an article in *National Geographic*, a transcript rarely shows to advantage. It can be disconcerting to read a transcript of one's own speech. I remember reading a transcript of a two-way conversation I'd had with another anthropologist, the first time I had ever read my own words. I was taken aback to discover how often I shifted focus and failed to complete an idea. Though both my colleague and I remembered the conversation as being exceptionally clear and focused, the transcript didn't reflect this (and from then on I resolved to follow a thought to its conclusion!).

Some basic methods of transcribing and of editing the transcript can aid the speaker unfamiliar with the sight of speech. I discussed these fundamentals in chapters 3 and 4; they include things such as using standard spelling, punctuating carefully, and deleting inessential nonwords (*um, er*). This is one time when the practice of editing out some of many false starts may be appropriate. You will still retain the full, unedited verbatim transcript for research use, and you still need to transcribe exactly what was said—after all, if there are to be changes, it is better that the speaker make them than you—but there are ways to polish that remain close to the verbatim version.

Participant reviews can be useful in clarifying content if that is the focus of the transcript. This is, after all, why oral historians carry out reviews. Even though speakers will be unable to reconstruct what they were saying if parts of the tape are inaudible, they can make many corrections of errors that you might not have noticed. You can also use the opportunity to resolve ambiguities or obtain missing information. If there are problematic pronouns, for example, flag them in the transcript and ask the participant to clarify them. If there are place-names or people that you need to pin down or would like to know more about, flag them, too. But this is a specific kind of ethnography, very much like oral history: your goal is an accurate narrative. It is inevitable that reviewing will change the unique, spoken style.

If you want try to retain the oral quality—that is, to prevent reviewers from changing the kinds of words used in speech rather than in writing—discuss this with them. Mention the fact that you want the transcript to sound "spoken"; explain that this style is more interesting to read and reflects real conversation. Words that signal oral exchange are often those that participants edit out.

If you have agreed with participants in advance that it is the contents of the final transcript and not those of the recording that are to be used by others, then this fact should be noted on the audio- or videotape and on the transcript itself. In one of my interviews, our formal agreement was that the participants would review and edit the transcript. We knew in advance that the interview would be sent to an archive and that the tape recording would not be the final version. We wanted to make sure that the tape was never considered the final version; to clarify this, when recording the formal opening of the interview, I began by announcing, "The final transcript is the final word, as there will be changes made to the verbatim transcript." The wording was not particularly felicitous—I devised it rather quickly at the request of the interviewee—but it conveyed the information that users should rely on and quote the transcript, not the tape, as the final text. The editorial changes in this interview were not radical, but they did clarify a few points, and the participants wished to make certain of their ability to ensure accuracy—and their control—from the beginning.

## PARTIAL TRANSCRIPTS

If you are publishing portions of, or quotes from, a transcript, you have the option of asking participants to review either the full or the partial transcript or the draft chapter or section of it in which parts of the transcript are quoted. You and the interviewee should have discussed the details of the review process and included them in your signed agreement or permission form. Many interviewers give participants a copy of the full transcript (whether or not a review of the whole transcript is requested), especially if it is to be put in an archive. Sometimes participants will request a copy of the tape as well.

If only a small selection of a transcript is being quoted, asking for a review of the relevant chapter or portion of a manuscript is both ethical and useful. In my experience, people tend to make many changes to full transcripts, only some of which are appropriate, whereas alterations to short quotations are usually pertinent and useful. The interviewee sees precisely what will be published and has a chance to correct his words (but not yours) if he wishes. This kind of review also takes less time, though here, too, you should specify a deadline. Since publication has its own deadlines, you might tell the reviewer that if you hear nothing from her, you will assume that the quotations are acceptable. This is not always sufficient: if you need the interviewee's input, you will need to wait for a response.

## VIDEO TRANSCRIPTS

In many projects, videos are shown side by side with the written transcript, or else the verbatim transcription text—with punctuation added and perhaps very lightly edited—runs across the foot of the picture. In a project in which videotapes are being transcribed for such a display, interviewees won't be reviewing the text but simply seeing what they said, and you will have explained all this to them before recording. In fact, few people object to their words on videotape—I believe this is because it *isn't* a written document.

## DISCUSSION TRANSCRIPTS

In some cases of recorded discussions, the discussants' role is finished with the recording. In other cases, discussants will take their work further by reviewing and using the transcript. Again, the intended use of the transcript will determine whether review is appropriate.

If participants are going to continue their discussion by means of transcripts, then theirs is a joint work, and everyone can address corrections of meaning. Perhaps you have made transcripts not so much for content as for other aspects of discussion—turn taking, speech styles, or context, for example. The decision whether to review will then be based on whether you are the sole analyst or whether the project is a joint one. In the latter case, you and the discussants or analysts will have a disciplinary regard for verbatim precision. Your joint responsibility will begin with the verbatim transcript, which may need to be changed, marked up, or annotated. Whatever the work, you share an understanding that it relies on a verbatim transcript.

Discussions recorded for publication are almost always jointly reviewed, and the kind of editing reviewers do will depend on whether the work is a book of philosophical argument, the minutes of a board meeting, or the ongoing comments of an informal discussion group. Grele's *Envelopes of Sound* is an example of a recorded discussion published as a book; the journal *Paris Review* is another such publication. In such cases—where it is content rather than aspects of oral exchange that is the focus—each discussant will be able to review and edit his or her part of the discussion. The rules for how participants are to do this (whether for clarity, meaning, style, or other attributes) will have been discussed and formalized in advance. Some publications, especially those discussing linguistic topics (such as Duranti and Goodwin's *Rethinking Context* [1992]), use partial transcripts to illustrate different points, and participants are not involved in the analysis. They may have seen transcripts, but the verbatim versions attempt to re-present much more than verbal content.

## PERFORMANCE TRANSCRIPTS

Many people and many goals are involved in the recording of performances. Transcribing the recording will bring all these into play, and each situation will have its own set of relationships, responsibilities, and review capabilities. The issue of intellectual property rights will surface as well. Once again I point you to Ruth Finnegan's discussion of ethics in her book *Oral Tradition and the Verbal Arts* (1992), particularly the section on intellectual property rights and the following comments (pp. 226–33). As she notes, transcribing is never routine but is an area in which "the researcher, as selector, formulator, translator, transcriber or presenter, is exercising power" (p. 232).

### What to Do When Reviewers Overedit

No matter how carefully you have described to participants the goals of your research and no matter how well you have explained to them the differences between oral and written speech, sometimes they will overedit a transcript as they review it—perhaps even altering its contents drastically. Whether you are bound to accept such changes depends partly on your prior agreement with the participants and partly on the uses to which the transcript will be put. Interviews and other material that will go in archives, as well as material to be published, are the kinds of transcripts most often subjected to review, and in these cases you will want to accept the changes made, at least for the final, "official" version of the transcript.

Sometimes, however, more creative solutions are called for when people edit too intensively. One thoroughly enjoyable interview I carried out related to the background history of a series of photographs of the building of a school. The participants were easy and pleasant to interview, and later I gave them a transcript to look over. When they returned it, I was surprised to find that virtually every third word had been altered. The editing did not change the facts, details, or general content of the narrative; they related more to style and perhaps stemmed simply from the urge to rewrite. My permission form had not specified how editorial changes would be handled, and I was unable—and frankly unwilling—to spend the time required to make the changes. So I placed both the (dated) original and the (dated and documented) reviewed version, with its handwritten edits, in a file along with the photographs. I noted on the later version that it had been edited by the interviewees. The interview was accurate, interesting, and engaging, whichever version was read, and I felt that this solution covered all ethical and practical bases.

If participants change their story or radically alter some points in a discussion, clearly you will need to make these changes, and this altered version will become the final version to be published or placed in a public archive. The changes themselves, however, may be of interest at some future point. The researcher (or project administrator) should always retain both the verbatim and the final version of any transcript of a recording. If at some later date these files are deposited in a public archive, there will be another opportunity to decide whether to cull the earlier version.

Sometimes participants have second thoughts about their interviews. They might regret what they have said about someone else, regret that they were asked to do the interview in the first place, or feel that they discussed a topic that should not have been mentioned. Unless publication has already taken place, there are various ways to handle such situations. The material can be cut from the final transcript altogether, and this (cut) version can be used or placed in an archive for public access. Or the original version can be placed in an archive with a restriction attached, stating that it cannot be used until after certain time period (this is common archival practice). Any material that goes into an archive can have restrictions placed on it. Discuss this option with participants. They may feel concerned about the present—hurting people's feelings or airing old grievances—but remain firmly committed to putting their thoughts down for the future. Last, and most radical, is neither to use the transcript nor to send it to an archive. In this case, it should not be kept but destroyed to prevent any use whatsoever. There is an excellent discussion of these matters and how archivists handle them in Sara S. Hodson's article "In Secret Kept, In Silence Sealed: Privacy in the Papers of Authors and Celebrities," which also mentions tapes and transcripts (2004, see p. 199).

## RESEARCHER AND USERS OF TRANSCRIPTS

When the transcription itself is completed to your satisfaction, you have its future life to consider. This future includes who, if anyone other than yourself, can or will use it and how they might best access the contents; where the transcript will repose after your own use—in your files, in a publication, or in an archive; and how any agreements, ethical constraints, or special needs are to be made known and enforced. You will need to decide whether to index the transcript, how best to preserve it, and how to cite it in publications when referring to it as a source document.

## Indexing Transcripts

Access to a document consists of having the ability to find and read it. Providing an index to a transcript makes it much more accessible than it might be otherwise, especially in the case of a lengthy interview or discussion. Indexing means additional work early on, but it will save you time in the long run, especially if you are analyzing and discussing several transcripts. Indexing also makes it easier for others to use the transcript in their own research. Oral historians often do extensive indexing of personal names, place-names, and topics discussed, referring to the tape as well as to the transcript by means of digital tape counters.

Even if the transcript is only for your own use, a few notes about the locations of specific items in which you are interested will always be helpful. You might produce an index using sophisticated software with that ability, you might use the "find" function in a word-processing program, or you might simply tag relevant pages with tabs that list the topic or topics discussed there.

If you need to index a transcript for broader use, however, your own index categories might not match others' interests or needs—and sticky notes will be insufficient, unprofessional, and unsuitable for archival preservation. In these cases you may need to enhance the index despite the extra time required. There are, of course, different levels at which to index. The first is the level of the individual transcript (and tape), the second the level of all transcripts within a project, and the third the level of all transcripts across projects. These levels apply both in your own work and in projects with many researchers. Index categories are names (including those of researchers, interviewers, and in some cases transcriptionists), events, places, dates, and topics you know are of special interest—to the research, to the project, and to any organizations or communities involved in producing or using the transcript. For large bodies of work, inventories are useful as well: lists of transcripts, their participants and researchers, and their dates, lengths, and locations. Computers make all such work somewhat easier and less time consuming.

This is not the place to tackle the methods or technologies for indexing, nor am I advocating that you do the extensive, skilled kind of indexing that is done for publications. But even minimal indexing—a listing of topics, names, dates, and places, with their page numbers—can give users quick, efficient access. If you have created computer documents, then users can search them by words or phrases, but supplying a list of terms used in the transcript will be helpful. If you used software to index transcripts for your own use, this may be problematic if there is limited access to the software or if it is expensive, dated, or simply not part of another institution's technology. If possible, print out the indexing terms you have used—you may have to add page numbers, depending on software—or, best of all, think ahead when using software to what may be printed out effectively in the absence of the software package.

Last, lest these suggestions overwhelm you, keep it simple. Indexing is a skill, but there is no need to let it take over. Those of us who enjoy creating databases and other such categorizing systems can easily get carried away, reducing everything to categories and fields. Names, places, and perhaps lists of a few basic key words are useful, even essential; beyond that, the transcript is a whole, not a series of sound bites.

*Preserving and Archiving Transcripts*

Whether or not you intend to place your transcripts, tapes, and notes in an archive, the question of preservation is relevant, even if it is only for the span of your own use. Magnetic media—audio- and videotapes—currently have a short shelf life, estimated at ten to thirty years, depending on manufacturer and how you store them. Computer hardware and software change and develop rapidly. Although there are many different ways to duplicate and maintain magnetic materials and computer technology, continual copying, reformatting, and upgrading is the norm, even in the personal computer system of an individual researcher.

## CREATE MATERIALS THAT WILL LAST

Materials created for any research project need to be produced with some attention to their life span in terms of both the materials from which they are made (magnetic tapes, paper) and the way in which they are stored, used, and maintained. For example, do not use original tapes, whether audio or video, for transcribing. This stretches the tapes and can even produce minor deletions in them. Every tape to be transcribed needs to be duplicated. This is best done with special equipment, but you can, in a pinch, create reasonably good-quality copy tapes by simply playing a tape on one tape recorder and recording it on a second (assuming that at least one of the recorders is professional equipment). You will need time and patience to do this and an environment without other noise.

Always use acid-free paper when printing out transcripts. Such paper is now inexpensive and easy to find—almost all office supply stores carry it; look on the package for the words "acid free." Photocopied materials can last well, depending on the type of machine and ink used. Acid-free folders—which are more expensive and need to be obtained from archival suppliers—are nice, but regular folders are perfectly adequate for short-term use (that is, anything under ten years). If you are scrupulously attending to the long-term preservation of research materials, use acid-free folders. For long-term preservation, do not write on folders or papers with "permanent marker" pens, which will bleed through layers of paper, or with ballpoint or other kinds of ink pens, which will fade over time. Store videotapes on end, like books, and keep all magnetic tapes boxed up in cool and preferably dark areas.

A useful source of information on topics in archival preservation for nonarchivists is the series of bulletins put out by the Council for the Preservation of Anthropological Records, which are available on a website maintained by the National Anthropological Archives (www.nmnh.si.edu/naa/copar/bulletins.htm). These bulletins focus on specific topics, among them "Easy Steps for Preserving Your Anthropological Records" (Bulletin number 3), "Preserving Audio-Visual Materials on Magnetic Tape" (Bulletin number 13), and "Creating Records That Will Last" (Bulletin number 14).

PROFESSIONAL ARCHIVES

If at some point you deposit, or consider depositing, your records in an archive, it's helpful to know how archivists will handle them. When a formal archival institution obtains collections, especially collections of tapes and electronic documents, the archivists will take certain normal steps—not necessarily immediately but within a few years, assuming they are well funded and staffed. They will professionally process and archivally house each collection and create finding guides in addition to whatever inventories and indexes accompany the collection (the finding guides may include online guides and inventories). Digital media, computer documents, and the relevant software require technological maintenance and, usually, reformatting—and the necessary funds, labor, and technical knowledge. Archivists may digitize some or all of your material, and they may update older technologies, but this will depend on funding and the professional standards, goals, and priorities of the institution. Undoubtedly, new technology will continue to enhance the life spans of all materials, especially the currently short-lived digital and video media. Paper always lasts, so whenever you can, maintain both paper and digital copies for long-term preservation.

Archival institutions operate with knowledge of their responsibility for copyright and intellectual property rights relating to use of their holdings. Archivists are cautious about allowing publication of transcripts that do not have permission forms. The current situation in terms of both copyright and intellectual property rights is murky, and often repositories simply state that the user is responsible for obtaining permission (for an interesting history of copyright, see Paul Goldstein's *Copyright's Highway* [1994]). They may provide direction and information to use in contacting people for permission. However, there are common archival practices to protect materials that may be libelous or damaging to living people or sensitive for them. One method is to accept documents but to keep them inaccessible for ten, twenty, or fifty years. If documents must remain closed to everyone forever, few archival repositories will accept them; what would be the point? And generally, archives are democratic, at least if they are publicly funded, and resist restricting access to a special group of people. There are, however, exceptions to this policy.

Last, it is worth noting that the demand for archival repositories far outdistances their number, funding, and professional capabilities. University archives, for instance, have huge responsibilities and equally large gaps in support. Investigate conditions at any institution to which you want to send records. If it is unable to manage what you feel your collection requires in terms of processing, preservation, and providing access, then consider obtaining help to undertake some professional processing beforehand. There are both grants and institutions that can assist you.

### Citation

Transcripts often need to be cited in reports and publications of many kinds. Especially if you are quoting passages from transcripts—yours or those of others—in your published work, you will need to choose methods for citing the sources of the quotations. Citations should be consistent and give readers the information they need to understand the source of the material being quoted or referred to (whether or not they can access the transcript itself). Style guides offer helpful, if incomplete, guidance.

If you are citing a published transcript, simply follow the guidelines in your chosen style manual for citing any published transcription or section of it; you need not identify the work as a transcript. For unpublished transcripts, style guides distinguish between several types, as follows.

The *Chicago Manual of Style*, 15th edition, discusses how to reference various forms of interviews, including transcripts (pp. 705–7; see especially section 17.205 on p. 705). It notes that the citation of a formal but unpublished interview should include "the names of both the person interviewed and the interviewer; brief identifying information, if appropriate; the place or date of the interview (or both, if known); and, if a transcript or tape is available, where it may be found. Permission to quote may be needed" (p. 705–11). Here, then, is the format:

> [Name of interviewee], interview by [name of interviewer], [date, place], interview number [if numbered], transcript, [archive information—name of institution, town, state].

Clearly, many references and citations will refer to unpublished transcripts in researchers' files. If the transcript is not publicly accessible, the archive information should read "unpublished transcript" or "unpublished data" (*Chicago Manual of Style* 2003:706–7).

If you publish extensive quotations from an unpublished interview (or any other type of unpublished transcript), there are several methods for citation from which to choose. In one of my own books (Powers 2001), I referenced each quotation from an interview in an endnote: name of interviewee, name of interviewer, and date of interview (a method I like but which one reviewer did not). The back matter included a list of all interviews (which were to be publicly accessible in a university archive) as a separate entry before the bibliography. Dennis Tedlock (1983), quoting from many of his own transcripts, always introduces the name of the speaker and the event, place, and date in the text, but he gives no reference citations except to those of his transcripts that exist in published form.

The *Publication Manual of the American Psychological Association* (1994:210) gives a format for citing written contributions to symposia, as follows:

> [Name(s) of person quoted]. [Date (include month)]. [Title of paper]. In [name of chair], [Title of symposium], symposium conducted at [institution or organization, and, if relevant, place].

The APA manual also gives a citation format for cassette tapes (p. 217):

> [Name], (Speaker). [Date]. [Title] (Cassette Recording no.___), [location of event: organization].

None of the formats suggested in these two style guides applies exactly to the kinds of recordings I have discussed in this book. Neither of them offers a specific format for citing discussions, whether in a symposium or at any other event, nor for transcripts of any recordings that are not interviews. To cite such sources, you will need to adapt the manuals' basic guidelines for interviews and unpublished materials, providing information that is relevant to readers who need to know what kind of unpublished material you are citing, when the event transcribed took place, where, and, if appropriate, under what kind of project or institution. You should also consider whether and when to list the names of participants in a citation; this will not be appropriate in all cases and is something to address when discussing permissions and ethics.

Several formats are possible:

1. Discussion, [names of participants if appropriate], [title of event if there is one, date, location], unpublished transcript [or, name and place of archive].
2. [Names of participants], discussants in [title of event, date, location]. Transcript in [location or "unpublished data"].
3. Discussion, [title of event, date, location]. Transcript, [location or "unpublished data"]

For focus group transcripts, you could retain "Discussion" or change it to "Focus group discussion."

Performances are another matter. The APA manual lists television broadcasts, series, and single episodes, but neither APA nor *Chicago* makes any mention of scripts or performances of any kind. In such cases it may be useful, in the interest of brevity, to cite more generally:

> Transcript of [performance or event title, place, date]. [Location of transcript or "unpublished data"].

Or, if you are quoting from a particular performer,

> [Name of performer], in [performance or event title, place, date]. [Location of transcript or "unpublished data"].

These are suggestions only. You may have better ones, or your discipline may have its own conventions. The point is to cite primary source material in a manner that is consistent and helps readers understand precisely where the quoted material came from.

## GOOD METHODS FOR USABLE TRANSCRIPTS

I have maintained throughout this book that ethnographers need standards and methods for transcription geared toward their disciplinary goals. Oral historians are concerned with the accuracy and quality of a transcript—hence the many guides for their work. Linguists need precision in annotation, for analysis of particular elements of speech and language. Knowing how and why your work is similar to, is different from, or overlaps with these two related approaches will allow you to choose an appropriate method. Those of us who record and transcribe in a way that highlights speech, its context, and its orality need to attend to good methodology and high standards, and we need to enlarge our tool kit to include them. A well-made transcript can be a document for the future. Though it will never exactly mirror the spoken word in all its creativity, social context, and ephemerality, the act of creating a transcript can teach us to listen to—and hear—this richness.

# APPENDIX A: SAMPLE FORMS

This section includes forms which may be used or adapted for use to efficiently guide transcription (form 1), formatting of transcripts (form 2), and introductory context material for each transcript (form 3).

## FORM 1: GUIDELINES FOR TRANSCRIPTION

Form 1 guides a verbatim transcription. The guidelines include points discussed in chapter 3, with options to select or cross out. Each element includes a section on "Special Instructions" that specifies what else is to be done. *Verbatim transcription: transcribe every word using this guideline*
*Goal of transcript:*

_____

_____

*Special Instruction:*

_____

_____

Conventional typographic symbols to be used in this transcript are listed on a separate page. Leave grammar exactly as spoken.

*Spelling:*
Use conventional spelling.
__ Use contractions: can't, don't, aren't, isn't, won't, ain't, and so on as heard
__ Use yeah, yup, and so on exactly as heard; OR _____

*Special Instructions:*
__ Spell words to represent sounds

---

*Language and dialect:*
Transcribe all words verbatim; spell unusual words (those not in dictionary) as they sound.
__ Use conventional spellings of all common words
*Special Instructions:* _____

*Punctuation of text:*
__ Use basic punctuation: periods, commas, question marks, em dashes.
__ Do not use colons or semicolons
__ Use exclamation points for _____
*Special Instructions:* _____

*False starts, broken sentences, repetitions of words:*
__ Include all false starts, broken sentences, repetitions
__ Use em dashes between phrases, repetitions, (do NOT use ellipses)
__ Omit repetitions of words
__ Use ellipses (three dots . . . ) only if speaker falters or seems hesitant
*Special Instructions:* _____

*Filler words* [example: "You know," "Like," "Obviously," or any phrase or word used frequently]:
__ Include all fillers
__ Omit fillers
*Special Instructions:* _____

*Nonverbal sounds:*
Assent and dissent sounds: uhuh [assent]; mhmhm [assent]; unhunh [dissent]
__ Include all; spell as above
__ Where relevant, follow each sound by [assent] or [dissent]
__ Include overlapping assent/dissent sounds of others, including those of the researcher:
    __ on a separate line
    __ in middle of speech as follows: word word word (Researcher: uhuh) word word word
__ Omit assent/dissent sounds of others, including researcher, in overlapping speech
__ Include assent/dissent sounds of researcher, omit others

Indicate the following nonverbal sounds—um, er, oh, ooh, mmm—as follows:
— Include all nonverbal sounds as above
— Do not include nonverbal sounds
*Special Instructions:* _____

Indicate other sounds such as laughter, coughs, sighs, and so on as follows:
— Use square brackets for the word, as follows [laughs], [coughs], [sighs], and so on
— Omit all sounds
— Laughter:
    — [laughs] if it is one person, [laughter] if it is more than one person
    — Time laughter as follows:
    [laughter .5 sec] — [laughter .5] — Other (specify) _____
    — Omit laughter; use exclamation point
*Special Instructions:* _____

*Pauses:*
— Use comma for pauses; otherwise do not include
— Indicate pauses as follows: [pause]
— Time pauses as follows: [pause 2 secs.]. Other notation _____
— Only note [pause] if pauses are longer than__ seconds

*Overlapping speech:*
When two or more people speak at the same time
— Transcribe, if you can hear the overlapping words, and indicate speakers if possible
— Start overlapping fragments on separate lines at point of overlap and use curly braces { } at the beginning and end of overlapping portion. Include names, unless you cannot distinguish speakers.
Example:    Jane: Oh    {the way it was then}
            John:        {we never knew how it} was then

*Unclear or hard to hear words or sections*
If you are uncertain of words/phrases, indicate as follows:
— Place the word(s) in square brackets preceded by a question mark; [?justice reigns]
— If you cannot decipher at all after a few tries, spend no more time, and:
    — Indicate by using square brackets that there are missing words, if possible giving approximate number of words/syllables. Do not write "garbled," "rubbish," or similar description.
    Example: [3 syllables unclear] [1+ words unclear] [cannot hear 2 words].

*Foreign language:*
Foreign words: The tapes include some words in _____
[list language(s)].
__ Do not transcribe; indicate as follows: [following word/phrase/section
in__ language]
__ Indicate tape counter of start of this section
__ Transcribe using italic font
Special Instructions: _____

*Researcher's speech*
__ Include researcher's introductory instructions
__ Omit researcher's introductory instructions as follows:
   __ Include first three words, indicate cut by ellipses in square
     brackets [ . . . ]
   __ Indicate entire omission by ellipses [ . . . ]:
__ Include researcher's comments and conversation
__ Omit researcher's comments and conversation as follows:
   __ Include first three words, indicate cut by ellipses in square
     brackets [ . . . ]
   __ Indicate entire omission by ellipses [ . . . ]

*Other sounds:*
__ Note interruptions (phones, people entering the room, other sounds that
   override speech) by brief description [phone rings] in square brackets.
Special Instructions: _____

*Note expressive aspects as follows:*
__ Include emphasis if words are emphasized strongly: use italic typeface
__ Do not include emphasis
__ Loud speech:__ indicate by capital letters; special instructions _____
__ Do not note loud speech
__ Soft speech: indicate by inserting [speaks softly]; special instructions ____
__ Do not note soft speech
Other _____

*Typographic symbols:*
Use the following conventional typographic symbols as indicated:
Parentheses ( ):
__ Do not use   __ Use for _____

Curly braces { }— Use when two or more people are speaking at the same time:

— Use curly braces at beginning and end of speech

Square brackets [ ]:

— Use when you insert any kind of comment

— Use if you have a query; type query in capital letters

— Use when you cannot hear words, noting if you can how many words are missing

— Use if you are uncertain about specific word(s) and precede with a question mark [?precede]

Question mark:

— Use for questions

Plus sign +:

— Use only when you are guessing at the number of words you cannot hear: [3+ words unclear]

Em dash:

— Use after false starts, broken sentences, repetitions

## FORM 2: FORMAT OF TRANSCRIPT

Form 2 gives practical details for the appearance and style of the transcript document.

Format the transcript as follows (all other details and methods of speech transcription listed separately):

Margins: Top _____ Bottom _____ Left _____ Right _____

Spacing: Double spaced _____ 1½ space _____ Single spaced _____

Font _____ Type size: _____

Number lines in transcript from the beginning: Yes _____ No _____

Justification: Left and right _____ Left only _____

Place page numbers at: _____

Running heads No ___ Yes ___ Content _____

Locate running heads at: _____

Title for first page as follows: _____

Give speakers' names as follows:

— Full name for each speaker, each time;

   — Name/initials in boldface— Name followed by a colon;

__ Initials of speaker after first speech __ in boldface __ followed by a colon
__ Last name only after first speech __ in boldface __ followed by a colon
Special Instructions: _____
Text format:
__ Name on left, all speech text indented from name
__ Speech text not indented, wraps from speakers name
Other _____
Special Instructions:
For italics _____
For boldface _____
For capitals _____
Use em dash as follows: dash—no space or dash — with space
Researcher should specify style for the following:
Numbers (see the *Chicago Manual of Style* for examples); Dates; Percentages;
Time;
Abbreviations and contractions: as speaker says them _____ Exceptions _____
If speaker mentions a common acronym write it : as commonly seen
(example)
Use: OK ____    O.K. ____    Okay ____
Preference for final transcript:
Word-processing program: _____
Put transcript on: Floppy disk _____    CD_____    Label as _____
Send document as attachment to _____
Number of hard copies required _____    No hard copy required _____
Special features, place-names, on tape: _____
Other instructions: _____

## FORM 3: DOCUMENTATION OF TRANSCRIPT

Form 3 outlines the basic information that should accompany a transcript.
More information can be given; this is the minimal information that provides
the context of the recording.
Transcript description/title: _____
Date of recording_____    Date of transcript _____
Project _____
Reason for recording _____
Participants _____
Shown in transcript as _____

Role/biographical details for each participant ⎯⎯⎯⎯⎯⎯⎯⎯⎯⎯⎯⎯
Researcher/interviewer ⎯⎯⎯⎯⎯⎯⎯⎯⎯⎯⎯⎯⎯⎯⎯⎯⎯⎯⎯⎯⎯
Role/biographical details ⎯⎯⎯⎯⎯⎯⎯⎯⎯⎯⎯⎯⎯⎯⎯⎯⎯⎯⎯⎯⎯
Location of recording ⎯⎯⎯⎯⎯⎯⎯⎯⎯⎯⎯⎯⎯⎯⎯⎯⎯⎯⎯⎯⎯⎯
Citation for transcript ⎯⎯⎯⎯⎯⎯⎯⎯⎯⎯⎯⎯⎯⎯⎯⎯⎯⎯⎯⎯⎯⎯
Other information ⎯⎯⎯⎯⎯⎯⎯⎯⎯⎯⎯⎯⎯⎯⎯⎯⎯⎯⎯⎯⎯⎯⎯

# APPENDIX B: TYPOGRAPHIC SYMBOLS USED IN NOTATION SYSTEMS

In this appendix, I list some of the traditional typographic symbols and conventions (such as underlining) used for punctuation and special treatment of words. In each entry, I first give the standard way in which the symbol is used in English-language publication, as recommended by, for example, *The Chicago Manual of Style* or the *Publication Manual of the American Psychological Association*. This is followed by a summary of some of the variant uses of the symbol found in transcripts and finally my recommended use and its rationale. When noting that a typographical convention should be reserved "for special use," I do not attempt to suggest any particular special uses. Rather, I leave it to others to develop special notations in the hope that eventually some consistent notations will be agreed on.

*Braces, Brackets.* See *Parentheses.*

*Colons.* While use of a colon as punctuation in a transcript would certainly not be wrong, I prefer to keep punctuation quite basic, in part because the constructions of speech simply don't match those of writing. However, colons are often used in transcripts to indicate a lengthened sound (for example, *oh:::*). This use of colons is, I think, a good one. Dennis Tedlock, in *Finding the Center* (1972), notes that repeating a letter to indicate drawn-out sound also runs the risk of appearing to change the sound (his example is that of extending the word "on" to ooooon). This can be handled in two ways: by care in which letter is repeated (for example, ooooh, and ohhhhh); or by using dashes (Tedlock's example is o--------n; the dash is joined and centered).

Recommendation: There is room for choice here. Colons can be re-served for special usage, which may include lengthened sound. You may want to use repeating letters, if you know that this is unlikely to be used for any other purpose. Dashes (that is, repeated hyphens) are useful when either pronunciation or indicating a more extended sound, as in oral narratives, is important.

*Em Dashes.* Writers frequently employ em dashes (—), which are the longest of three kinds of standard dashes used in English-language publishing, the other two being en dashes (–) and the common hyphen. Publication style guides give many uses for em dashes: for explaining, in place of a comma, for parenthetical remarks, and for sudden breaks. Transcriptions are inconsistent and vary broadly in their usage of em dashes. Em dashes and ellipsis points have been used interchangeably to show repeated words, false starts, breaks, and pauses.

Recommendation: Use em dashes for false starts, incomplete sentences, breaks, and so on within a sentence. Do not use them for pauses; instead, write [pause].

*Two-Em Dashes.* Two-em dashes are, as the name implies, the length of two em dashes together. They are usually typed as four hyphens in a row: ----. They are used to indicate a missing word or part of a word—that is, a segment that cannot be clearly heard. As mentioned previously, they can indicate lengthened sound.

Recommendation: Use them for a word left out intentionally, for example, when omitting a name for privacy. While this may appear to be similar to cutting out material, for which ellipsis points are used, the reason for the omission is different. Two-em dashes could also be used to indicate extended sound in a word. When words cannot be heard, make it clear (for example, [inaudible words]) rather than using a two-em dash.

*Ellipsis Points.* In publishing, three dots or ellipsis points are used to indicate that material has been intentionally cut out in a quote (*Chicago Manual of Style*, 2003:458–59; *Publication Manual of the American Psychological Association*, 1994:245). However, the *Chicago Manual of Style* also uses ellipsis points for faltering speech, speech that is "accompanied by confusion, insecurity, distress, or uncertainty," noting that "the dash, on the other hand, suggests some decisiveness and should be reserved for interruptions, abrupt changes in thought, or impatient fractures of grammar" (p. 368). The American Psychological Association does not address faltering speech—hardly a concern in the preparation of manuscripts for professional research articles, papers, or books.

In transcripts, ellipsis points have been used to indicate pauses, in incomplete sentences, and for false starts. They have also been used to indicate stammers: y..y..yes. Note that dashes are also used for exactly the same range of notations. I think it is necessary to establish some consistent usage. A few points are in order. I think it is a grave mistake to indicate pauses by ellipsis points; it is not sufficiently clear. Pauses, interruptions of speech (decisive or indecisive), and cut or omitted material are three entirely different entities; they should be represented clearly. Distinguishing between more decisive changes in thought (using em dashes) and indecisive or faltering speech (using ellipses), as suggested by the *Chicago Manual of Style*, is quite difficult, especially in false starts, but should it be necessary to show faltering speech, there needs to be a notation for it.

Recommendation: Use ellipsis points in square brackets for omitted material. Though I do not feel that there is always sufficient evidence for "indecisive" faltering speech as opposed to "decisive" false starts and broken sentences, when it is useful to show this difference, use ellipsis points without square brackets. Do *not* use ellipses for broken phrases, false starts, or pauses. If you want to indicate stammers, use hyphens: y-y-yes. If you are studying stuttering, you may have or want to develop a better or more formal way to note this, especially if you want to be able to search a document electronically for such appearances of stutters.

If your work is later quoted or, more important, if you yourself want to quote from a transcript and omit some material, by using ellipses in brackets [ . . . ], you will want to be able to indicate cuts clearly.

A note on omitting material: if, in the final transcript, you decide to omit certain words—for example, filler words or false starts—I do not recommend using ellipses. I have suggested using ellipses in a verbatim transcript when you omit more extensive material, such as a researcher's instructions or comments. Whether you indicate such cuts in a final transcript is up to you. However, note that in quoting from a transcript in which such cuts are indicated as well, perhaps, as further cuts for the quotation, the ellipses [ . . . ] will not distinguish the original cuts from later cuts. I do not think this matters very much.

*Exclamation Points.* The *Chicago Manual of Style* notes that exclamation points mark "an outcry, an emphatic or ironic comment" and recommends "sparing" use. The APA manual does not mention them at all; humor or outcry probably does not play a large role in such publications.

Recommendation: Use in a transcript to indicate that a speaker is joking, recognized from tone of voice or content, or laughing. Use exclamation points to mark ironic comments. Other emphatic comments, or outcries, could be noted differently, for example, by underlining for emphasis, using capitals for loudness, and, if necessary, adding a context comment.

*Slashes (Forward Slashes).* It is standard practice in writing to separate alternatives by slashes (he/she, either/or), and they could be used for the same purpose in the spoken word, though alternatives spoken in this way might be rare or at least limited. Backward slashes are reserved for computer conventions. In transcripts, slashes have been used to indicate overlapping speech, to indicate a pause, or to show rising or falling tones. Linguistic notation sometimes uses them to denote phonemes.

I suggest that slashes be reserved for special uses (such as linguistic notation) and recommend that they *not* be used for overlapping speech (see *Curly Braces*) or pauses (see *Square Brackets*).

*Hyphens.* Use hyphens to separate characters, if for example, a speaker is stammering or spelling something out or perhaps running a group of words together.

*Parentheses ( ), Square Brackets [ ], Curly Braces { }, and Angle Brackets < >.* These are all useful symbols in transcript notation, and they are used freely, if inconsistently, and with a high degree of individual choice on the part of analysts. I recommend specific usage for square brackets and curly braces, suggest one for parentheses, and leave some room for special purposes.

*Parentheses.* Publication style guides have many uses of parentheses: for explanatory phrases that are less directly related to the content of a sentence and a host of other uses related to bibliographic references, citations, indexes, and mathematics. These are not particularly relevant to transcription. While speakers do make unrelated or digressive comments, transcriptionists generally do not place such comments in parentheses. This would go quite far in the direction of reading a speaker's intentions. Parentheses should be used for other purposes.

There seems little agreement on what this purpose should be. In some transcripts, parentheses set off context comments. In others, they are used to insert an assent sound or short response made by another speaker in the midst of the main speaker's talk. Sometimes, they indicate speech that cannot be heard clearly, in which case there may be either a few partial words or a blank space within the parentheses. They are used for pauses, often with a number indicating seconds (2.0) inside the parentheses. Many transcripts use parentheses for all the previously mentioned notations, and since these are all in effect context comments, this is consistent. In addition, parentheses have been used to show overlapping speech or to indicate an accompanying gesture. Some researchers use double parentheses (( )) to indicate added material.

Recommendation: Use single parentheses for inserting an assent or very brief remark made by another speaker, for example, an interviewer, in the middle of a speech:

AG: Though it was long ago, I haven't forgotten. (Interviewer: Uh-huh) No sir, I won't forget it, not ever. (Interviewer: I'm sure.) It's as clear in my mind as yesterday.

Reserve double parentheses for special needs, one of which might be to indicate gesture. Do not use them for pauses or any other comments or context notes added to transcripts. Instead, use square brackets (see the next section). Overlapping speech can be show by curly braces (discussed later).

*Square Brackets [ ].* In publishing, these are used consistently to indicate material inserted by a third person, such as the editor; this usage is widespread. (Publishing makes several additional uses that are not relevant here.) Square brackets are indeed often used in transcripts to indicate material inserted by someone other than the original speaker(s), usually the researcher in an editorial capacity or the transcriptionist who has queries. Note also that square brackets are used in phonetic transcription.

Recommendation: Use square brackets to indicate anything added to the original speech. This includes pauses, whether timed [2.0] or not [pause]; descriptive words; a phrase to indicate that words cannot be clearly heard; and context comments. So, for example, the following would all be inserted in brackets: [laughter], [phone rings], [speaker points to the window], [unclear word]. Square brackets should also be used when the transcriptionist cannot hear words clearly and they are thus uncertainly transcribed or are inaudible and not transcribed at all. When a word is uncertainly heard, either enclose it in square brackets with a question mark [forward?] or follow it with a notation in square brackets: forward [?unclear]. If words are quite inaudible, indicate by a phrase: [cannot hear 3 words] or [1+ inaudible words/syllables]. The logic governing all of these uses is that they contain material that is inserted by an outside party.

If a transcriptionist has any queries to the researcher, he could insert them in square brackets—or in angled brackets. Typing queries in capital letters can be useful for visibility since they will be removed eventually.

*Curly Braces { }.* In publishing, these are used only for special purposes (providing examples in mathematics).

In transcription, curly braces { }, parentheses ( ), and square brackets [ ] are all used by different writers to indicate overlapping speech. Legal transcriptionists typically use parentheses.

Recommendation: I suggest that curly braces be used for overlapping speech, when two or more people speak at the same time. If you can hear the overlapping words, place the brace at the point where joint speech begin and again where the overlap ends. Typically, this overlapping speech is printed on two lines, as follows:

Sarah: If I pull this drawer out, {you can see what's} inside.
Jane:                              {No, don't do that}

Often when transcribed overlapping speech is published, the curly brace or a square bracket is elongated vertically to encompass both lines. This clarifies the overlap, and the braces look quite different from those produced by computers. Transcriptionists will need to use the computer for the unpublished versions of transcripts; curly braces are symbols that have no competing usage.

*Angle Brackets* < >. These play a role in editorial preparation of manuscripts for electronic typesetting. They are conventionally used to indicate greater than (>) and lesser than (<) in mathematical equations. There is an etymological use as well (< for "derived from" and > for "gives" or "has given").

Recommendation: Reserve for special usage, which may include the previously mentioned uses.

*Question Marks*. These are, of course, used for questions in publications. In transcripts where tone and pitch are noted, question marks have been used to show rising tone. They are always used to indicate unclear words or segments.

Recommendation: Use question marks for questions and, in combination with square brackets, to annotate those words that you cannot be sure of, for example [?in confrontation with]. Usually, question marks are placed before the uncertain word or phrase, but they could be used both before and after them. Do not use to indicate tone, pitch, or other special uses.

*Quotation Marks*. In publication, they are used for quoted words or phrases, for direct speech, for "unspoken discourse" (or not, as the writer prefers), but not for interviews, indirect speech, and dramatic scripts (see *Chicago Manual of Style*, 15th ed., pp. 453–58). They suggest that words can also be marked by placing them in quotation marks. *Chicago* notes that "scare quotes . . . are often used to alert readers that a term is used in a nonstandard, ironic, or other special sense" (p. 293). The APA manual suggests using quotation marks for introducing ironic words or invented expressions and dropping the quotation marks after the first use. Often, slang or colloquial terms are placed in quotation marks, single or double; they need not be. In fact, there is a general overusage (not to mention inaccurate usage) of such quotation marks.

Recommendation: Quotation marks should be left to your discretion. People often report the speech of others. You can enclose this in (double) quotation marks if you choose, or you can set reported speech off by commas. Speakers may quote well-known sayings or poetry or other things, and again, the use of quotation marks is optional (note that such quotations may not be perfectly accurate). You could use single quotation marks perhaps for words that are somehow marked, ironically or in some other way, *by the speaker*. Do not put the speaker's terms or words in quotation marks simply because it is nonstandard usage in writing. Use quotation marks only if you can hear their irony or if perhaps they indicate by gesture some marking of words—in which case you will have to make a note for an audiotaped version. These are subtle distinctions but important ones. Better to omit quotation marks unless you have a good reason to include them.

*Underlining and Italics.* In publications, underlining is used for bibliographic entries and other elements not relevant to transcripts. Italic typeface is commonly used in publications to indicate emphasis, foreign words, scholarly words, and terms in specific contexts (as well as very specific uses in indices and bibliographies). In transcripts, either italic typeface or underlining is used to indicate words the speaker says emphatically. However, italic typeface is also used 1) for contextual comments, usually placed in parentheses, and 2) to indicate the original language, in a transcript with an interlinear translation. Sometimes it is not used for any of these elements.

Transcripts also show emphasis by accent marks or sometimes by capital letters. But capital letters have been used to indicate volume, accent marks a rising tone, and so on. Consistency is hard to agree on because different research will examine different clusters of elements. Researchers also need to note co-occurring features; for example, those who study tone will want to mark not only emphasis but a range of changing voice tones as well.

Rather than making recommendations, I will try to pull out the common conventions and suggest what might be basic and what remain free for usage.

*Italic Typeface.* Typically, this indicates emphasis, and if used in a transcript, this is usually clear when italics is not used for any other purpose. However, italics are and should be used in transcripts in which a language and its translation are shown side by side. The original language is usually in italic and the translation in roman. If a speaker uses one word or many in another language (code switching), this too is usually indicated by italics. Some transcriptionists use italics, as mentioned, to indicate editorial comments or "script" comments.

*Underlining.* Transcriptionists often use underlining in transcripts to show emphasis. This too seems clear. A few transcripts use underlining for rising intonation or for loudness.

Both italics and underlining seem to be used for the same purposes. But transcripts that focus on several features of speech that appear simultaneously may need underlining and italics. Italics are consistently used to show words in another language. In interlinear translations, one language—usually the original language—appears in italics and the translation into English in roman. When speakers code-switch, put those words in italics. However, should emphasis be needed in either of these language uses, the transcriptionist can indicate this simply by underlining. And, when context comments in square brackets are also in italics, this begins to look like overuse.

Using italics when working with two languages in a transcript is useful and virtually universal. Underlining may thus be the best way to consistently mark emphasis in either typeface. In this way, various features can be identically noted in each language (and can extend also to the following discussion of capital letters and type size).

*Boldface.* This appears to have no particular meaning in publication other than as a design element. In transcripts, too, it appears as a design element (for example, to set out the names of speakers). There are additional though less common purposes, including noting emphasis or marking a specific segment or word for analysis or attention.

Recommendation: Reserve boldface either for design or for special use (they are unlikely to coincide or confuse). Do not use it for emphasis.

*Capital Letters.* Publication style guides do not encourage the use of capitals for emphasis except in rare cases. Many researchers use capital letters to indicate loud speech in transcripts, and this convention seems both clear and practical. Capital letters are also used in linguistic transcription for grammatical notation, inserted in abbreviated form and not in parentheses of any kind, but often hyphenated to a word or stem. These two uses do not coincide and are unlikely to be confusing.

Recommendation: Use capital letters for loud speech where sound is important. Other common usage that does not coincide can be continued.

*Different-Sized Type.* In transcripts, size of type (in addition to capital letters) is sometimes used to indicate sound. Quiet speech is placed in small typeface, loud in capital letters, and shouting in enlarged capitals, and computers can do this handily. This seems to be common usage among those who transcribe performance, poetry, or even plain speech.

A sloping line of text appears in some transcripts to indicate rising or falling intonation (see, for example, Dennis Tedlock's [1972] work). This is something that can be done on a typewriter but is difficult to do on a computer, though it is possible to drop by lines.

However, other transcripts indicate volume by comments [spoken quietly] [said very loudly] instead. I have also seen degree symbols (°) used to mark quiet speech.

Recommendation: Smaller typeface seems useful for quiet speech. If it is not possible to do this, introduce quiet speech by a context comment in square brackets [spoken quietly]. If you can create sloping type for falling or rising tone, this seems useful. Otherwise, I leave it to those who need to indicate tone and intonation to build on the basic notations here.

# APPENDIX C: SAMPLES
# OF TRANSCRIPTS

## EXAMPLES OF TRANSCRIPTS WITH DIFFERENT GOALS

The following examples illustrate something of the range of transcripts and the different elements that may be necessary for analysis. They also suggest the variety of notation systems to illustrate the usefulness of consistent shared symbols. For instance (see example 2), I think it is clearer and more obvious when the times of pauses are given right in the transcript. Transcripts can be simple, but they often need the ability to indicate certain aspects of speech. A basic system provides shared conventions and still leaves many symbols free for specialized use without confusing a reader.

*Example 1*

This is a basic verbatim transcript and is part of the initial research for a book. It is punctuated, not edited, and has no context comments. This is the section from which I took excerpts to quote in *Navajo Trading: The End of an Era* (Powers 2001:141–42).

EF:   We took that store and, of course, my great love was the arts and crafts, I was fortunate and lucky enough to find a manager, Ken Matthews from down here, and his love was livestock.

WP:   Oh, so he took the livestock.

EF:   And so we took that store together and probably had more fun at that during about a ten to fifteen year period; we were buying, at one time, almost a third of the wool on the reservation.

WP:   On the whole reservation?

EF:   On the whole reservation.

WP:     You were really doing a big wool trade.

EF:     Well, we would ship to Johannesburg, to France and England. Well, we had fun. The livestock we were buying—and it just got to be to where we were doing—and that we had what I call every door in that trading post working at full-bore: the livestock; the arts & crafts; and the front door with groceries.

WP:     Wow! How many stores did you have at that point?

EF:     One.

WP:     Just one?

EF:     My theory was if I concentrated—Shiprock was in such an area that the population was there that you could make that as big as you wanted to work. And I always figured I was ahead concentrating on one over several small ones. And we took that store to probably be, volume-wise, probably at that time by far the largest store on the reservation, by volume.


*Example 2*

This excerpt is from Aaron V. Cicourel, "The Interprenetration of Communicative Contexts: Examples from Medical Encounters" (p. 297 in Duranti and Goodwin [1992], reprinted with the permission of Cambridge University Press). This excerpt illustrates several things. It shows a particular format, with numbered lines, initials and colons for speakers, and speech text fully indented. There are many context comments in square brackets (here, [abrupt shift]; in the full transcript, voice level is annotated in this way too). It illustrates yet another method of showing overlapping speech (| at the beginning of the overlap and indentation). There is a stammer and a phonetic spelling. The two dots in line 30 each indicate, as per the author's key, a pause of one second. In other words, the pauses are timed but shown as dots.

| 23 | PA: | So she didn't have peripheral, evidence of shock |
|----|-----|---------------------------------------------------|
| 24 |     | Really? \|Just a low blood pressure.              |
| 25 | MR: | \|No, she wasn't, she wasn't ever clamp, you      |
| 26 |     | know                                              |
| 27 | PA: | OK                                                |
| 30 | MR: | I can..and, and she doesn't                       |
| 31 |     | [abrupt shift] one thing that argues              |
| 32 |     | against a lot of neuropathy, you know, from diabetes, for |
| 33 |     | one, she's only had it for three years, but two, you know, |
| 34 |     | her neuro exam an' her peripheral vascular exams, |
| 35 |     | is really normal, is normal sensory, good pulses distally, |

36       and stuff, and I just have a hard time,
37  PA:  Yeah
38  MR:  there'd be a lot of sy-sympathetic, you know
39  PA:  Right
40  MR:  phone calls.


## Example 3

This excerpt, from Tullio Maranhão, "Recollections of Fieldwork Conversations" (p. 281 in Hill and Irvine, [1992], reprinted with the permission of Cambridge University Press), illustrates two languages, in side by side translation, and his notation of gesture by the use of parentheses and short dashes. Note also the use of ellipsis dots in brackets indicating an omitted passage. Maranhão gives a short key at the start of the transcript.

| | |
|---|---|
| *chegue ali (---) do* | I arrived there (---) on that site |
| *Calá pra lá* | of Calá |
| *ele já ia indo acolá em* | he was already going there below |
| *baixo (---), na beira da* | (---) by the edge of the beach |
| *praia* | |
| *mais na frente–* | further ahead— |
| *"sabe que eu vô"* | "you know, I'm going" |
| *aquela vontade de ir . . .* | that desire to go . . . |
| *aí só fiz descer* | then all I did was go down |
| [. . .] | |
| *cheguei lá naquela pedra* | I arrived there at that rock (---) |
| *(---), que tem na rumada* | that there is in that grove of |
| *acolá (---)* | coconut trees there (---) |


## Example 4

This example, from Jane H. Hill and Ofelia Zepeda, "Mrs. Patricio's Trouble" (p. 199 in Hill and Irvine [1992], reprinted with the permission of Cambridge University Press) illustrates code switching, in which inserted words are shown in italics, with the translation given in capital letters located exactly underneath the original. These (capitalized) words do not appear to have been said by the speaker, although it is not absolutely clear—some people who code-switch do say the words in both languages. It would help to place them in square brackets, but in this transcription, nonwords have been placed in brackets.

1. ...We've been,
2. *gdhu haha 'I ha'ap ki:*
   JUST LIVING RIGHT OVER THERE
3. in town all this time
4. until two years ago [mhm]
6. That's why *mo g ñ-,*
   WHY MY,
7. *ñ-ma:mad pi ho:hoid 'iya'a [ooh]*
   MY CHILDREN DON'T LIKE IT HERE...
8. They come,
9. but they wanna go back into town cause[


*Example 5*

This excerpt, from Charles Goodwin and Marjorie Harness Goodwin, "Assessments and the Construction of Contexts" (p. 156 in Duranti and Goodwin [1992], reprinted with permission of the Cambridge University Press), illustrates only a few of the quite extensive notations the authors required for analysis and for which they give a key. Note the use of double parentheses plus italics for context comments, boldface for emphasis, asterisk plus "hh" for inbreathing, a degree sign to indicate that what follows is in lower volume, colons showing lengthened sound, and dashes showing the sudden cutting off of sound. The brackets halfway between lines show the beginning of overlapping speech.

(1) Paul:    Tell y- Tell Debbie about the dog on the
             ((*smile intonation begins*)) golf course t'day.
    Eileen:  °eh hnh ┌**hnh** ha has! ┌Ha!
    Paul:           └**hih** hih    └Heh Heh! *hh hh
    Eileen:  *hh An this beautiful, ((*swallow*))
    Paul:    I rish Setter. ((*reverently*))
    Eileen:  [Irish Setter
    Debbie:  ah:::,


*Example 6*

This excerpt is from the author's own transcript of a symposium discussion held at the Wheelwright Museum. Names of discussants are given in the original; here I have used initials.

Friday morning October 24, 2003 **Session 1**
*[Tape 3 Side A]*
*Audience member:* I've had one jeweler tell me to put unpolished silver in the sun. Have you ever heard that?
*BB:* For what reason?
*Audience member*: It helps polish it. I've heard jewelers say that.
*BB:* Any members of the panel on that one?
*Voice [unidentified]*: Sun worshiper! Sounds strange to me.
*BR:* Bob, could you look at this one wrist guard, there. Do you see that as a similar issue of that white surface? I just found that one very raw looking, again. I described it kind of critically, but—
*BB:* Yes. Raw is perhaps a good word. The surface of the silver is very different from, say, this one. This is polished and shiny, all right, where this one is—the surface is not as reflective. And yet it is not tarnished, it's not black, it's not blue or brown, it's kind of white, the way you expect silver to be but it's a—it's almost like a white dusty surface. [ ... ]
*MBR:* What is "German silver"—does it tarnish like regular silver?
*BB:* Well, German silver is copper, nickel and zinc, so there's no silver in it.

# REFERENCES AND FURTHER READINGS

Basso, Ellen B. 1985. *Kalapo Myth and Ritual Performance*. Philadelphia: University of Pennsylvania Press.

Basso, Keith. 1972. "To Give up on Words": Silence in Western Apache Culture. In *Language and Social Context: Selected Readings*, edited by P. P. Giglioli. New York: Penguin Books.

Baum, Willa K. 1995. *Transcribing and Editing Oral History*. Walnut Creek, CA: AltaMira Press.

Bauman, Richard. 1986. *Story, Performance, and Event: Contextual Studies of Oral Narrative*. Cambridge: Cambridge University Press.

Berlin, Ira, Marc Favreau, and Steven F. Miller, eds. 1998. *Remembering Slavery: African Americans Talk About their Personal Experiences of Slavery and Emancipation*. New York: The New Press in association with the Library of Congress.

Burlings, Robbins. 1992. *Patterns of Language: Structure, Variation, Change*. New York: Academic Press.

*Chicago Manual of Style: The Essential Guide for Writers, Editors, and Publishers*. 15th ed. 2003. Chicago: University of Chicago Press.

Clifford, James. 1988. *The Predicament of Culture: Twentieth-Century Ethnography, Literature, and Art*. Cambridge, MA: Harvard University Press.

Council for the Preservation of Anthropological Records (CoPAR). *Guide to Preserving Anthropological Records*. www.nmnh.si.edu/naa/copar/bulletins.htm

Duranti, Alessandro. 2003. Language as Culture in U.S. Anthropology: Three Paradigms. *Current Anthropology* 44, no. 3: 323–47.

Duranti, Alessandro, and Charles Goodwin, eds. 1992. *Rethinking Context: Language as an Interactive Phenomenon*. Cambridge: Cambridge University Press.

Fine, Elizabeth C. 1984. *The Folklore Text: From Performance to Print*. Bloomington: Indiana University Press.

Finnegan, Ruth. 1992. *Oral Tradition and the Verbal Arts: A Guide to Research Practices*. London: Routledge.

Frank, Gelya. 2000. *Venus on Wheels: Two Decades of Dialogue on Disability, Biography, and Being Female in America*. Berkeley: University of California Press.

Freedman, Don, and Jacqueline Rhoads. 1987. *Nurses in Vietnam: The Forgotten Veterans*. Austin: Texas Monthly Press.

Fromkin, Victoria. 2000. *Linguistics: An Introduction to Linguistic Theory*. Oxford: Blackwell Publishers.

Giglioli, Pier Paolo. 1972. Introduction. In *Language and Social Context: Selected Readings*, edited by P. P. Giglioli. New York: Penguin Books.

Goffman, Erving. 1983. *Forms of Talk*. Philadelphia: University of Pennsylvania Press.

Goldstein, Paul. 1994. *Copyright's Highway: The Law and Lore of Copyright from Gutenberg to the Celestial Jukebox*. New York: Hill and Wang.

Gone, Joseph P. 1999. "We Were Through as Keepers of It": The "Missing Pipe Narrative" and Gros Ventre Cultural Identity. *Ethos: Journal of the Society for Psychological Anthropology* 27, no. 4: 415–40.

Goodwin, Charles, and Alessandro Duranti. 1992. Rethinking Context: An Introduction. In *Rethinking Context: Language as an Interactive Phenomenon*, edited by A. Duranti and C. Goodwin. Cambridge: Cambridge University Press.

Goody, Jack. 1987. *The Interface between the Written and the Oral*. Cambridge: Cambridge University Press.

Grele, R. T. 1985. *Envelopes of Sound: The Art of Oral History*. 2nd ed. Chicago: Precedent Publishing.

Hill, Jane H., and Judith T. Irvine. 1992. Introduction. In *Responsibility and Evidence in Oral Discourse*, edited by J. H. Hill and J. T. Irvine. Cambridge: Cambridge University Press.

Hodson, Sara S. 2004. In Secret Kept, In Silence Sealed: Privacy in the Papers of Authors and Celebrities. *The American Archivist* 67, no. 2: 194–211.

Hymes, Dell. 1981. *"In Vain I Tried to Tell You": Essays in Native American Ethnopoetics*. Philadelphia: University of Pennsylvania Press.

Ives, Edward. 1995. *The Tape-Recorded Interview: A Manual for Field Workers in Folklore and Oral History*. Knoxville: University of Tennessee Press.

LeCompte, Margaret D., and Jean J. Schensul. 1999. *Analyzing and Interpreting Ethnographic Data*. Ethnographer's Toolkit, vol. 5, edited by J. J. Schensul and M. D. LeCompte. Walnut Creek, CA: AltaMira Press.

Maranhão, Tullio. 1992. Recollections of Fieldwork Conversations, or Authorial Difficulties in Anthropological Writing. In *Responsibility and Evidence in Oral Discourse*, edited by J. H. Hill and J. T. Irvine. Cambridge: Cambridge University Press.

Powers, Robert P. 2005. Two Pueblo Perspectives on the Pajarito Plateau: An Interview with Julian Martinez, San Ildefonso Pueblo, and Joseph Suina, Cochiti Pueblo. In *The Peopling of Bandelie: New Insights from the Archaeology of the Pajarito Plateau*, edited by R. P. Powers. Santa Fe, NM: School of American Research Press.

Powers, Willow Roberts. 2001. *Navajo Trading: The End of an Era.* Albuquerque: University of New Mexico Press.

*Publication Manual of the American Psychological Association.* 4th ed. 1994. Washington, DC: American Psychological Association.

Ritchie, Donald A. 1995. *Doing Oral History: A Practical Guide.* New York: Twayne Publishers.

Schegloff, Emanuel A. 1992. In Another Context. In *Rethinking Context,* edited by A. Duranti and C. Goodwin. Cambridge: Cambridge University Press.

Schensul, Jean J., Margaret D. LeCompte, Bonnie K. Nastasi, and Stephen P. Borgatti. 1999. *Enhanced Ethnographic Methods: Audiovisual Techniques, Focused Group Interviews, and Elicitation Techniques.* Ethnographer's Toolkit, vol. 3, edited by J. J. Schensul and M. D. LeCompte. Walnut Creek, CA: AltaMira Press.

Schensul, Stephen L., Jean J. Schensul, and Margaret D. LeCompte. 1999. *Essential Ethnographic Methods: Observations, Interviews and Questionnaires.* Ethnographer's Toolkit, vol. 2, edited by J. J. Schensul and M. D. LeCompte. Walnut Creek, CA: AltaMira Press.

Silverstein, Michael. 1996. The Secret Lives of Texts. In *Natural Histories of Discourse,* edited by M. Silverstein and G. Urban. Chicago: University of Chicago Press.

Sturtevant, William C., gen. ed. *Handbook of North American Indians.* Washington, DC: Smithsonian Institution.

Tannen, Deborah. 1994. *Talking from 9 to 5: How Women's and Men's Conversational Styles Affect Who Gets Heard, Who Gets Credit, and What Gets Done at Work.* New York: William Morrow.

Tedlock, Dennis, trans. 1972. *Finding the Center: Narrative Poetry of the Zuni Indians.* Lincoln: University of Nebraska Press.

———. 1983. *The Spoken Word and the Work of Interpretation.* Philadelphia: University of Pennsylvania Press.

Tilley, Susan A. 2003. "Challenging" Research Practices: Turning a Critical Lens on the Work of Transcription. *Qualitative Inquiry* 9, no. 5: 750–73.

# INDEX

Adair, John, 24
ambiguous pronouns, effect on meaning in editing oral speech, 70–71
*Analyzing and Interpreting Ethnographic Data, Volume 5* (LeCompte and Schensul), 4
angle brackets, 116
archiving transcripts, 97
assent sounds, 49
"Assessments and the Construction of Contents" (Goodwin and Goodwin), 124

Basso, Ellen, 80
Basso, Keith, 15
Baum, Willa, 19, 27
Bauman, Richard, 77
Berlin, Ira, 19
boldface, 118
brackets, 115

capital letters, 118
"'Challenging' Research Practices: Turning a Critical Lens on the Work of Transcription" (Tilley), 35
*Chicago Manual of Style*, 34–35, 46, 85, 112–13
*Chicago Manual of Style*, 15th edition, 3, 35, 111, 116

Cicourel, Aaron, 122
citations: cassette tapes and, 100–101; ethical issues and, 101; focus group transcripts and, 101; performances and, 101; published transcripts and, 99–100; symposia contribution of, 100; unpublished transcripts and, 100
Clifford, James, 16
code switching, 56
colloquial words, 44
colons, 35
communication, forms of, 15–16
context, kinds of, 74
contextual information, 74–81; basic details of, 75; editing and, 61; ethnographic methods and, 62; importance of, 74; introductory information and, 74–75; locale features and, 76; notes, importance of, 62; photographs and, 77; voiced audience interaction and, 79
copyright, 77
*Copyright's Highway* (Goldstein), 99
Council for the Preservation of Anthropological Records (CoPAR), 27, 98

131

# ABOUT THE AUTHOR

**Willow Roberts Powers** is an anthropologist with a Ph.D. from the University of New Mexico who lives and works in Santa Fe, New Mexico. She writes, coordinates special programs for the Wheelwright Museum of the American Indian, and consults for a variety of small groups and Native American communities interested in cultural heritage programs, oral history projects, and archives. She has published two books on Navajo trading that draw on interviews, and she continues to do research that depends on interviews and their transcripts.